DISCOVERING AN EVANGELICAL HERITAGE

Discovering
An Evangelical
Heritage

Donald W. Dayton

HARPER & ROW, PUBLISHERS

New York, Hagerstown, San Francisco, London

FIRST EDITION

Designed by Stephanie Krasnow

Library of Congress Cataloging in Publication Data

Dayton, Donald W
    Discovering an evangelical heritage.
    Bibliography: p.
    1. Evangelicalism—United States. I. Title.
BR1642.U5D39 1976   269′.2′0973   75–36750
ISBN 0–06–061781–0
ISBN 0–06–061780–2 pbk.

76 77 78 79 80 10 9 8 7 6 5 4 3 2 1

To
GILBERT MORRIS JAMES
Professor of the Church in Society,
Asbury Theological Seminary,
and creator of
the Urban Ministries Program for Seminarians,
whose life has been dedicated to keeping alive
the spirit of the Evangelical heritage here
discovered and whose influence has helped
midwife and nurture the insights of this book

Contents

Acknowledgments

To the editors of the *Post-American* (now *Sojourners*) for permission to use material that first appeared in their pages in different form as a ten-part series entitled "Recovering a Heritage," published from June–July through May 1975.

To my brother, Deane Dayton, who allowed me to enter his darkroom and watch as he turned stained nineteenth-century engravings into the sparkling prints used to illustrate this book.

To my wife, Lucille Sider Dayton, who allowed me to mine jointly authored studies on the history of Evangelical feminism for materials used in this book.

Prologue:
On Coming to Maturity in an
Evangelical College in the 1960s

Whether the fact is admitted or not, most books arise out of the author's personal history. This book is no exception. In an age perhaps excessively conscious of the subliminal influence of social and psychic history on one's thinking and sensitivities, fairness to the reader requires frankness about the life situation behind one's writing. This book is a product of the author's struggle to reconcile the seemingly irreconcilable in his own experience: the Evangelical heritage in which he was reared and values bequeathed him by the student movements of the 1960s.

The cultural trauma of the 1960s is now the common heritage of all America—and much of the world! That decade saw wave after wave of social protest and the emergence of new movements for justice and equality: the civil rights movement with its sit-ins, freedom rides, marches, confrontations, and deaths; the great revulsion against the Vietnam War expressed in protest, draft resistance, draft-card burnings, exiled youth, and conspiracy trials; and the discovery of unnoticed minorities and a history of neglect and oppression that tarnished the images of the United States on which we had been nourished in grade school. Few would defend today all that happened in the 1960s, but most would allow that in that decade fundamental principles came to light that can no longer be ignored. There is no going back to the innocence of the 1950s.

There was, however, in the 1960s at least one relatively safe bastion of escape from this turmoil—the subculture that despite its diversity is encompassed by the label "Evangelical." The basic transmitters of this tradition are a series of "Christian

colleges" (some independent and some denominationally an-
chored). These schools, usually situated in rural, small-town, or
suburban locations, are scattered across the country but tend to
cluster in the Midwest. They are not widely known, but their
names (Wheaton, Houghton, Malone, Greenville, Seattle Pacific, etc.) are revered within Evangelicalism as fortresses
against the modern world, in which Evangelical youth can be
educated and mate without threat from the pagan ideologies and
life-styles of the secular world.

It is difficult to recreate the atmosphere of such a college in
the 1960s. No doubt the incidents that loom so large in memory
were not the whole of campus life. But the contrast between the
pettiness of the issues that troubled us and the magnitude of the
issues that were being dealt with in society is frightening. Campus life was circumscribed by cultural patterns and ethical
mores called "prudentials" at my college. These included the
traditional Evangelical prohibitions against drinking, smoking,
dancing, card-playing, and theater-going. Our lives were largely
bound up in testing the limits of these prohibitions. While other
students responded to calls for civil rights workers or took to
the streets in protest about Vietnam, we fought our administration over whether the yearbook could picture male swimmers
without T-shirts, struggled for the right to watch TV in the
lounge on Sundays, and wondered if the Christian should attend
the theater (legitimate or cinema) or read twentieth-century
literature.

We tended to be apolitical, but when political instincts did
surface, they were conservative. Like most Evangelicals of the
decade, we supported Richard Nixon and Barry Goldwater in
presidential elections. I was aware of only one voice of dissent
on campus, a rather moderate Democrat who was harassed into
leaving over his "liberal" political views and questionings of the
campus ethos. Our great fear was communism, and we found
signs of its influence everywhere. We believed that the protest
movements were manipulated by Communist agitators. Our editorial complaints that the campus lacked sufficient diversity for
the dialogue that was an essential part of any liberal education
were interpreted as the first steps in a campaign to bring a

Communist speaker to campus or even to start a Communist cell.

Cultural insularity and reactionary social perspectives converged to produce what John Oliver of Malone College has termed "A Failure of Evangelical Conscience."[1] Evangelical Christianity rather consistently opposed currents of the 1960s that demanded social justice and civil rights. John Oliver has traced this through the editorial pages of *Christianity Today*, the journal that spoke for Evangelicalism in that decade. Claiming to represent the "biblical point of view," the editors defended "voluntary segregation," charged of Martin Luther King that "communism . . . is implicit in his integrationist ideology," condemned categorically demonstrations and civil disobedience, decried as a "mob spectacle" the 1963 March on Washington at which Martin Luther King delivered his famous "I Have a Dream" speech, praised Mississippi's refusal to admit black student James Meredith to its state university, and were horrified at the suggestion of interracial marriage. Concerning the war in Vietnam, the editors supported the American presence, stating that it was necessary for the security of Christian missions. They rebuked the critics of the war and called for the enforcement of laws against destroyers of draft cards and records while insisting that justice be "tempered with mercy" for those convicted of war crimes. They denied that the United States had any economic or other "ulterior motives" for its presence in Indochina. The journal, of course, altered its position on most of these issues, but only in response to a reversal of popular consensus or official national policy.

The full significance of this "failure of Evangelical conscience" has yet to be understood. To many of us, the civil rights movement and its principles of fundamental human equality seemed not only more right, but more biblical and Christian than the positions taken by our elders. We learned

1. John Oliver, "A Failure of Evangelical Conscience," *The Post-American*, May 1975, pp. 26–30. To keep scholarly apparatus to a minimum, only material from modern, secondary literature has been documented. The bibliography indicates the major sources consulted in the preparation of each chapter.

that what had been claimed as biblical and therefore absolute was often the deification of cultural patterns not only relative but in some cases even pernicious and demonic. Sizable contingents of several generations of Evangelical college students responded to these insights by leaving the orbit of Evangelicalism. Those that did not abandon the Christian faith altogether have found places of service in other parts of the church.

The trauma generated by these conflicts was intense. Torn between Evangelicalism and the imperatives of the civil rights movement, I chose the latter—though troubled with a continuing "bad conscience" acquired through years of conditioning in the Evangelical world. I worked with the Mississippi Freedom Democratic party in the election of 1964. I lived with blacks on the edge of Harlem during the riots of the summer of 1964 and identified in successive years with various black churches and inner-city ministries. Cut loose from Evangelicalism, I threw myself into the secular education of Columbia University and went to Yale Divinity School, seeking a theological reconstruction that could bring my intellectual world back together. In several years of study and experience I found that reformulation in the recovery of a biblically grounded and classically Christian faith amenable to the development of social responsibility—and even a biblically grounded "Christian radicalism."

Having established an independent standpoint, I was able to look back on Evangelicalism with some equanimity. In what was intended to be a casual aside in a graduate program in theology, I took up the study of the roots of the denomination in which I had been reared. Though never helped to understand its history in college or in church life, I discovered much to my surprise that the denomination was a product of the closest parallel to the civil rights movement in American history—the abolitionist protest against slavery in the pre–Civil War period. The founders of my denomination and college were advocates of principles in which I had come to believe by a very indirect route. As I pursued this story, I discovered the sweet irony that this denomination was not unique, but shared a reformist heritage with other aspects of Evangelicalism. I had been struggling with the wrong end of Evangelical currents that had once reverberated with vitality and reform activity, but had over the course of a century fallen into a form of decadence. This book is an overview of that history—a history that has forced me to rethink, not only my own relationship to Evangelicalism, but the broader significance of that movement in American culture.

1   Jonathan Blanchard: The Radical
Founder of Wheaton College

If there is a single symbol of modern Evangelicalism, it is Wheaton College, situated just to the west of Chicago in the "All-American City" of Wheaton, Illinois. This school of about two thousand students is the most prestigious and perhaps the oldest of the "Christian colleges" that lie at the core of Evangelical culture and tradition. The city of Wheaton is itself a mecca for Evangelicals. Headquartered here and in the surrounding area are many of the publishers, independent mission boards, and interdenominational agencies that compose the network of Evangelical life and activity. Also in Wheaton are the offices of the National Association of Evangelicals, an "ecumenical" organization founded in 1942 that today draws together some thirty denominations in an Evangelical counterpart to the National Council of Churches.

Closely associated with the post–World War II Neoevangelical renaissance of scholarship that spawned the National Association of Evangelicals, Fuller Theological Seminary in Pasadena, and *Christianity Today*, Wheaton College is the alma mater of many leaders of contemporary Evangelicalism. Among these are Harold Lindsell, editor of *Christianity Today*; the late Edward J. Carnell, Fuller apologist and philosopher of religion; and Carl F. H. Henry, founding editor of *Christianity Today*. But the most famous alumnus of Wheaton College is evangelist Billy Graham, class of 1943. Through his position on the board of trustees and in other ways Graham is still a dominant force in the life of the college—as in all of the Evangelical world.

Billy Graham has rather consistently expressed what may be taken to be the position of the National Association of Evangelicals, *Christianity Today*, much of Wheaton College, and most of the Evangelical world: that the primary mission of the church is the spiritual one of preaching a gospel of "personal salvation" through faith in the atonement of Christ. Social witness may be an extension of the life of the individual regenerated person in society but should not be incorporated into the life of the church as a primary goal.

Graham expressed this position in a "clarification" issued early in 1973. When the peace negotiations in Paris broke down and the United States resumed its bombing of North Vietnam, a number of American churchmen appealed openly to the evangelist to use his friendship with President Richard Nixon to try to stop the bombing. In his response Graham said:

I am convinced that God has called me to be a New Testament evangelist, not an Old Testament prophet! While some may interpret an evangelist to be primarily a social reformer or political activist, I do not! An evangelist is a proclaimer of the message of God's love and grace in Jesus Christ and of the necessity of repentance and faith. My primary goal is to proclaim the Good News of the Gospel of Jesus Christ. The basic problem of man is within his own heart. That is why evangelism is so important.[1]

This position is generally assumed to be what Evangelicals have always believed. To some extent this is true. But while Billy Graham sometimes uses the language of repentance and faith to avoid questions of social responsibility, earlier generations of Evangelicals understood that repentance involved turning from apathy into the heart of struggles for social reform. While Billy Graham contrasts the "New Testament evangelist" and the "Old Testament prophet," earlier Evangelicals combined these roles. One of the most significant figures of that earlier generation was Jonathan Blanchard, the founder of Wheaton College.

The central building on the Wheaton College campus is Blanchard Hall. At the top of a split winding staircase just inside the main entrance are two plaques honoring the men for whom the building is named. These men are Jonathan Blanchard and

1. Billy Graham, "A Clarification," *Christianity Today*, 19 January 1973, p. 36.

Charles A. Blanchard, father and son, the first and second presidents of Wheaton. These two men held the office for over twenty and forty years, respectively. Together they guided Wheaton College through its first sixty-five years.

Each plaque contains a quotation that calls into question the Evangelical perspective expressed by Billy Graham. On the plaque honoring Charles Blanchard is an affirmation of the reformist aspiration of youth.

The need of a developing nation is to increase in wisdom, righteousness and strength and to cast off whatever is inconsistent with that noble age to which youth aspires. Only that which is true and right can abide. (From an address on the Day of Prayer for Colleges, "The American College")

More striking is the quotation on the plaque honoring Jonathan Blanchard, the founder of Wheaon College. It is taken from an address entitled "A Perfect State of Society," originally delivered before the Society of Enquiry during the commencement exercises of Oberlin College in 1839. (The significance of Oberlin will emerge later, in chaps. 4 and 5.) The plaque reads:

Society is Perfect where what is right in theory exists in fact; where Practice coincides with Principle, and the Law of God is the Law of the Land.

This passage is the thesis of Blanchard's address in which he treated "not so much the principles of the doctrines of Christ, as the form they will give society, when they have done their perfect work upon mankind." Among the affirmations of Blanchard at Oberlin was that "every true minister of Christ is a universal reformer, whose business it is, so far as possible, to reform all the evils which press on human concerns." Blanchard fully realized that one "cannot construct a perfect society out of imperfect men," but argued that "every reformer needs a perfect state of society ever in his eye, as a pattern to work by, so far as the nature of his materials will admit."

This somewhat utopian vision was grounded in a doctrine of the kingdom of Christ reflected in the Wheaton College motto, "For Christ and his Kingdom." Blanchard understood the king-

dom of God as "Christ ruling in and over rational creatures who
are obeying him freely and from choice, under no constraint but
that of love" and argued that what "John Baptist and the Sav-
iour meant when they preached the 'kingdom of God' " was "a
perfect state of society." He opposed those who emphasized
that such a kingdom is not to be sought in this world, insisting
that though "this kingdom is not *of* this world, it is *in* it."
Carrying this affirmation to its logical conclusion, Blanchard
warned against both those who "locate Christ's kingdom in the
future to the neglect of the present" and those who seek "to
construct a local heaven upon earth, . . . thus shutting out the
influences and motives of eternity."

Prompted by this vision of a "perfect state of society" and
compelled by obedience to Christ's command to "seek ye first
the kingdom of God," Blanchard was propelled into a life of
reform that climaxed in the founding of Wheaton College. His
life was so dominated by reform that upon his death the *Political Dissenter* commented that "in the death of Dr. Jonathan
Blanchard, American reformers have lost one of their foremost
leaders. No more fearless voice ever rang out on the platform,
or from the pulpit. No keener or more valiant pen has been
wielded against popular wrongs, and in defense of unpopular
truth."

Born in Vermont in 1811 and a graduate of Middlebury
College, Blanchard studied theology at Andover Theological
Seminary. There he came under the influence of Theodore Weld
(for the significance of Weld, see chap. 3) and became, in the
words of the *Dictionary of American Biography*, a "violent
abolitionist." When the administration of Andover tried to stop
his antislavery work, Blanchard withdrew and spent a year in
Pennsylvania working as an agent for the American Anti-Slavery Society. (Agents were "agitators" who traveled around lecturing and organizing local chapters of abolitionists.) Blanchard
endured mob violence, threats on his life, and other forms of
abuse in this work. He then finished his education at Lane
Theological Seminary in Cincinnati where he continued his
abolitionist activities. Upon graduation he was called to pastor
Cincinnati's Sixth Presbyterian Church, a congregation widely

known as the "nigger church" for its abolitionism. In spite of Blanchard's reformist orientation, the church added during his seven-year pastorate some five hundred members to the original one hundred and twenty.

Blanchard's commitment to reform soon propelled him into an important leadership role among the abolitionists. He held office in the Ohio Anti-Slavery Society. In 1843 he was elected to the American vice-presidency of the World's Anti-Slavery Convention in London. In 1845 he was called upon to represent the Cincinnati Abolition Society by debating against N. L. Rice the affirmative of the proposition that "'slaveholding is in itself sinful and the relationship between master and slave a sinful relationship." This debate, in Cincinnati's largest auditorium and lasting several days, was widely advertised and published in a five-hundred-page book that went through several editions. This work is so important for understanding the abolitionist movement that several modern publishers have reprinted it as a major resource for black studies programs.

After this debate Blanchard carried his reform ideas and work into education. For twelve years he served as president of Knox College in Galesburg, Illinois. After controversy forced his resignation, he was offered the presidency of a half-dozen other colleges, but he eventually accepted the position at Wheaton. This school had actually been started in 1848 as Illinois Institute by the Wesleyan Methodists, an abolitionist body that had split from Methodism in 1843 over the question of slavery. (See chap. 7 for a discussion of the Wesleyan Methodists.) A few years later the Congregationalists joined the Wesleyans in support of the young institution, and when the Wesleyans failed to muster sufficient financial support, the college was rechartered in 1860 under Congregational control.

This change was made only after a covenant that Wheaton would continue Wesleyan reform principles. These were expressed in an advertisement for the college that appeared in 1859, vowing to preserve

the testimony of God's word against slave-holding, secret societies and their spurious worships, against intemperance, human inven-

tions in church government, war, and whatever else shall clearly
appear to contravene the kingdom and coming of our Lord Jesus
Christ. . . .

Jonathan Blanchard was one person that all could agree upon to
be president of the college. His reformist temperament promised
the continuation of the ideals upon which Wheaton was to be
established. Blanchard accepted the invitation, and, as he put it
himself, "I came to Wheaton in 1860, still seeking 'a perfect
state of society' and a college 'for Christ and his Kingdom.' "
And to Wheaton he gave the rest of his life.

Blanchard grounded his vision for the Christian college in the
prophetic texts of Scripture. He pointed to the "schools of the
prophets" where the "ancient people of Jehovah sent up their
youth to learn the pure principles and practical application of
his law." In those schools, according to Blanchard, the "truth of
God" was explained to young "prophets" who were to see that
this truth was "faithfully applied to correct the follies and the
errors of the nation."

Blanchard's position on reform can best be understood
through an examination of the Cincinnati debate. He affirmed
the radical equality of the slaves in these words: "I rest my
opposition to slavery upon the one-bloodism of the New Testament. All men are equal, becaused they are of one equal blood."
He argued that slavery was a sin to be immediately abolished
and suggested that church discipline be brought to bear upon
those who held slaves or supported the institution of slavery. He
did not view the question of slavery as an individual matter of
personal purity, but insisted that "slave-holding is not a solitary,
but a social sin," deserving attack on all fronts.

But we must also understand the position of his opponent,
N. L. Rice. Though Blanchard attempted to brand him an advocate of slavery, Rice insisted that he, too, was an abolitionist,
but committed to gradual abolition and "colonization" (sending
the slaves back to Africa). He feared that the radical abolitionists were pushing too hard and were "upturning the very foundations of society in order to abolish slavery." He expressed

concern for the "spiritual welfare" of slaves and slaveholders. He argued that if Southern ministers should become abolitionist, they would be expelled and all would be left without the "preaching of the gospel." Rice was concerned that the minister not move too far ahead of his congregation.

Blanchard insisted that Rice's position made his "religion . . . the religion of a privileged class" by perpetuating an evil system. Blanchard maintained that the churches and individual Christians must radically identify with the oppressed and wished after his death to be remembered only as "one who having humbly striven in all things to follow his Lord, like Him, also has been faithful to His poor" (Blanchard's final words in the Cincinnati debate).

Controversy still rages over whether the abolitionists were misguided fanatics or clear-sighted moral reformers. Earlier historiography dismissed them and bewailed their tendency to bring into the arena of public policy moral absolutes that could not be accommodated to the compromises of political solutions. Sensitized by the 1960s recent scholars have taken a more sympathetic look at the abolitionists and have discovered one of the most profound reform movements in American history—a movement that was largely grounded in Evangelical Christianity.

But whatever modern American historians may decide about the abolitionists, it is clear that Blanchard was completely on their side. He called the abolitionists "honest, simple-hearted, and clear-sighted; but few of them dwellers in high places; who take up the truth and the cross with it, to bear both after Christ." Indeed, he went so far as to identify the early Christians as "a poor despised set of abolitionists who were everywhere accused of 'uprooting society' to get rid of its evils, and *'turning the whole world upside down'* to correct its errors and reform its abuses."

The debate between Blanchard and Rice was not between an abolitionist and a proslavery defender of the status quo, but between two divergent strategies for the elimination of slavery. Rice viewed Blanchard as an extremist upsetting the gradual process of amelioration of slavery effected by the preaching of the gospel, while Blanchard viewed Rice as a compromising equivocator unwilling to act on the radical implications of the gospel. To use more modern terminology, it would appear that Jonathan Blanchard, the founding president of Wheaton College, was, at least on the issue of slavery, a radical rather than a liberal.

2 Reform in the Life and Thought of Evangelist Charles G. Finney

Jonathan Blanchard, however, was not a lone voice for reform in his age. He was part of a much larger movement that combined the roles of "New Testament evangelist" and "Old Testament prophet." Wheaton College was only one manifestation of a revival movement that reached back to the pre–Civil War evangelism of Charles G. Finney, the father of modern revivalism. The Blanchards were among his disciples, and Wheaton College understood itself to stand in his succession. As late as the 1940s and the 1950s V. Raymond Edman, Wheaton's fourth president, called the Evangelical world back to Finney as "the most widely known and most successful American revivalist."[1] Edman's book, *Finney Lives On*, carried an endorsement by Billy Graham.

Charles Grandison Finney, however, was greater than either the secular caricature of a ranting, hell-fire evangelist or the Evangelical images of a deeply spiritual preacher given totally to the "saving of souls." In the words of American historian Richard Hofstadter of Columbia University, he "must be reckoned among our great men."[2] Though first and foremost an evangelist, Finney's work and the way he understood the gospel "released a mighty impulse toward social reform"[3] that shook the nation and helped destroy slavery.

1. V. Raymond Edman, *Finney Lives On: The Secret of Revival in Our Time* (Wheaton, Ill.: Scripture Press, 1951), p. 15.
2. Richard Hofstadter, *Anti-Intellectualism in American Life* (New York: Alfred A. Knopf, 1964), p. 92.
3. Gilbert Hobbs Barnes, *The Anti-Slavery Impulse 1830–1844*, reprint edition with new introduction by William G. McLoughlin (New York: Harcourt, Brace and World, 1964), p. 11.

Born in 1792 in Connecticut, Finney was reared in central New York in what has come to be known as the "burned over district"—so called because "revival fires" so often swept the area. After two years of education in a Connecticut academy, he returned to upstate New York to study, and eventually to practice, law. Well on his way to a successful legal career, Finney began to study the Bible to better understand law-book references to Mosaic legislation. The result of this reading (and the prayers and entreaties of his fiancée) was a spiritual struggle climaxing in a profound conversion. The morning after his initial religious experience, Finney announced a new vocation to a startled client: "Deacon, I have a retainer from the Lord Jesus Christ to plead his cause and I cannot plead yours."

At the age of twenty-nine Finney began informal study for the ministry. Within a few years he was ordained and was gaining a national reputation as an evangelist through his work in upstate New York. By the early 1830s Finney was preaching to large crowds in Philadelphia, Boston, and New York. In 1835 he published his *Lectures on Revivals of Religion*, reissued in a 1960 critical edition by Harvard University Press as a determinative force in the shaping of American culture. Also in 1835, Finney was invited to become professor of theology at the newly founded Oberlin College. Except for frequent revival trips to New York, England, and elsewhere, Finney spent the rest of his life in Oberlin, becoming president of the college in 1850.

Controversy surrounded Finney's work on several levels. He introduced into revivalism many "new measures" that shocked more conservative evangelists. His preaching style was popular and colloquial, though forceful and laced with the logic of the lawyer. He popularized the "protracted meeting" that continued for several days or weeks and employed the "anxious bench," a row of seats in the front of the church for those under "conviction" of sin. Perhaps the most controversial of his "new measures" was encouraging women to pray and speak in "promiscuous" or mixed assemblies.

But the content of Finney's preaching was as troubling to conservatives as his methods. Revivalism is generally understood in terms of the dramatic conversion of profligate sinners, but such an image is not true to the literal meaning of "revival." Finney's message was directed primarily to church people or "professors of religion" not living up to the fullness of Christian existence. The revival was a means of "breaking the power of the world and of sin over Christians." This involved the accusation that many (perhaps most) church people were less than vital Christians, a suggestion vigorously resisted by the traditional clergy. But this call to a "revived" Christian life incorporated the implicit demand that true conversion evidence itself in good works and commitment to the welfare of others. In such dynamics is the beginning of an impulse to reform activity.

Finney also generated controversy by his repudiation of "Old Calvinism" that discouraged human effort and created a certain "aristocracy of the elect." He vigorously denounced the old doctrine of election and denied that one must wait for the "miracle of conversion" that God would bring about according to divine discretion—or not at all. Finney argued that God wills that all should be converted and receives all who turn from their sin. This implied a new role for the human will and a new emphasis on human ability. When this doctrine was transposed into the social sphere, it meant that God had given men and women a role in the shaping of society and that nothing had to be accepted as it was.

Certain other features of Finney's thought moved him in the direction of egalitarianism. Finney affirmed not only that all may be saved but that the fundamental fact about a person is human sin and the need of conversion. Lifting such convictions to determinative principles resulted in a profound "leveling" effect that produced a "Christian egalitarianism" congenial to the emerging Jacksonian affirmation of the value of the common person. Lyman Beecher, a more conservative revivalist from New England, disliked the democratic Western revivalists who implied that "all men, because sinners, are therefore to be treated alike by ministers of the gospel without respect to age or station in society." Here are the seeds of a very basic egalitarianism, which was later to bear fruit in abolitionism and feminism.

For Finney the essence of sin was selfishness. Such concern

for one's own welfare was directly contradicted by God's character, especially the attribute of benevolence. To be "converted" for Finney was to forsake one's own interests for the sake of others. This reflection of God's benevolence in the life of the convert would evidence itself in "doing good" to all and becoming as "useful" as possible in the world. The natural outlet in Finney's time for such impulses was a series of "benevolent societies" set up for every conceivable philanthropy and social crusade. Finney's converts threw themselves into such work.

Finney himself made conversion central and was never willing to substitute reform for revival, but he did make the reforms an "appendage" to revival. In discussing the slavery issue, for example, the evangelist wished to make "abolition an appendage, just as we made temperance an appendage of the revival in Rochester." By this connection Finney preserved the centrality of revivals while still promoting reforms and propelling his converts into new positions on social issues.

This conjunction of reform and revival was also reversible. Finney not only argued that revivals should produce reforms, but also that resistance to reform was one of the great "hindrances of revival." In his *Lectures on Revivals of Religion* Finney argued that "revivals are hindered when ministers and *churches take wrong ground in regard to any question involving human rights.*" He applied this particularly to slavery, insisting that "the church cannot turn away from this question." He argued that "the silence of Christians upon the subject is virtually saying that they do not consider slavery as a sin" and claimed that "it is vain for the churches to resist for fear of destruction, contention, and strife" or to "account it an act of *piety* to turn away the ear from hearing this cry of distress" from the "shackled and bleeding" slaves.

Finney even argued that if the church fails to speak out on such an issue "she is perjured, and the Spirit of God departs from her." In effect, he insisted that the spiritual vitality of the church is sapped, not by her involvement in social questions, but rather by her failure to embrace reform. In Finney's own words, "One of the reasons for the low state of religion at the present time, is that many churches have taken the wrong side on the subject of slavery, have suffered prejudice to prevail over principle, and have feared to call this abomination by its true name." Finney went on to call for the use of church discipline on the *social* sin of "slaveholding." Since it is impossible for the church "to take a neutral ground on this subject," while she "tolerates slaveholders in her communion SHE JUSTIFIES THE PRACTICE." Though Finney refused to disrupt the church practices of others, he affirmed that "where I *have authority*, I exclude slaveholders from the [Lord's Supper], and I will as long as I live."

Finney, however, is not honored for such convictions today by Evangelicals. Modern editions of his works are often expurgated. Offending passages are removed, leaving the impression that Finney avoided moral and ethical disputes for the sake of the "spiritual." V. Raymond Edman's book *Finney Lives On*, for example, contains a synopsis of the *Lectures on Revivals of Religion* listing only twenty-two of twenty-four "hindrances to revival" in the original edition. Omitted are references to "resistance to reform" and "taking the wrong ground on questions of human rights." The remaining "hindrances" are renumbered with no indication that Finney claimed that the spiritual vitality of the church may be destroyed from within by failure to take a stand on social issues.

But an even more egregious example of such censorship is found in *Revival Fire*.[4] This volume contains "letters on revivals" originally published in the *Oberlin Evangelist*. They represent Finney's mature thought and were written to deal with the emotional excitement that accompanied revivals and the failure of converts to continue in the Christian life. One of the most striking of the original letters was entitled "The Pernicious Attitude of the Church on the Reforms of the Age." This title is retained in the modern editions of *Revival Fire*, but the content of the letter that follows is entirely different! The letter printed treats the problem of "excitement."

The original text of that letter follows. Though lengthy, it is

4. This book has appeared in several twentieth-century editions. The most recent reprint is in the Dimension Books paperback series published by Bethany Fellowship of Minneapolis.

Finney's most stirring statement on the relationship of the church to reform. It has been completely excised from the modern editions of the letters and is now available in only a very few surviving sets of the original *Oberlin Evangelist*.

LETTERS ON REVIVALS—No. 23   By Prof. Finney

The Pernicious Attitude of the Church
on the Reforms of the Age

To all the Friends and especially all the ministers of our Lord Jesus Christ:

Dear Brethren:

There is one subject upon which I must remark further, and yet I fear it will be impossible to do it justice without giving offense. One of the most serious impediments that have been thrown in the way of revivals of religion and one that has no doubt deeply grieved the Spirit of God is the fact that the church to a very great extent has lost sight of its own appropriate work and has left it in a great measure to be conducted by those who are for the most part illy prepared for the work. The work to which I refer is the reformation of mankind.

It is melancholy and amazing to see to what an extent the church treats the different branches of reform either with indifference, or with direct opposition. There is not, I venture to say upon the whole earth an inconsistency more monstrous, more God-dishonoring, and I must say more manifestly insane than the attitude which many of the churches take in respect to nearly every branch of reform which is needed among mankind.

To such an extent is this true that scarcely a church can be found in the land which as a body will have anything to do with reform. Hence the only way in which Christians in the churches who would do any thing towards reforming mankind can make their influence felt is by forming societies, composed often partly of Christians and partly of those who profess no religion. These unite together to concentrate their influence against some form of iniquity that is cursing mankind.

Now the great business of the church is to reform the world— to put away every kind of sin. The church of Christ was originally organized to be a body of reformers. The very profession of Christianity implies the profession and virtually an oath to do all that can be done for the universal reformation of the world. The Christian church was designed to make aggressive movements in every direction—to lift up her voice and put forth her energies against iniquity in high and low places—to reform individuals, communities, and governments, and never rest until the kingdom and the greatness of the kingdom under the whole heaven shall be given to the people of the saints of the most High God—until every form of iniquity shall be driven from the earth.

Now when we consider the appropriate business of the church— the very end for which every Christian vows eternal consecration, and then behold her appalling inconsistencies everywhere apparent, I do not wonder that so many persons are led to avow the solemn conviction that the nominal church is apostate from God. When we consider the manner in which the movement in behalf of the slave has been treated by ecclesiastical bodies, by missionary associations, by churches, and ministers, throughout the land, is it any wonder that the Church is forsaken of the Spirit of God?

Look at the Moral Reform movement. A few devoted, self-denying females, engaged in a mighty conflict with the great sin of licentiousness. This struggle has been maintained for years; and yet how few comparatively of the churches as such have treated this effort in any other way than with contempt. A few devoted Christian women in various churches form societies to aid in this work; but where are the churches themselves as a body? Where are these sworn reformers—these men and women who profess to be waging everlasting war against every form of sin? Where are the ministry? Do they lift up their voice like a trumpet? Do they cry aloud and spare not? Do they as John Adams says, thunder and lighten from their pulpits, every Sabbath against these sins?

It is amazing to see what excuses are made by ministers for remaining silent in respect to almost every branch of reform.

And pray what can be meant by the sickening cry of moral suasion? The Church with a great many ministers have resorted to the plea of using moral suasion as the means of ridding the world of intemperance, licentiousness, slavery and every other legalized abomination; but pray what can be meant by moral suasion? Moral Government surely is a system of moral suasion. Moral suasion includes whatever is designed and adapted to influence the will of a moral agent.

Law, rewards, and punishments—these things and such as these are the very heart and soul of moral suasion. It would seem as if a great many people mean by moral suasion nothing more than flattery and palaver. Consequently when efforts are made to secure legislation that shall put these abominations away, they are afraid to employ government lest it could be a departure from the system of moral suasion. But is not God's government one of moral suasion? Are not his mighty judgments on the one hand and his mercies on the other, moral suasion?

But not to dwell on the subject of moral suasion; the idea I wish to present to the brethren is this—the great sin and utter shame of the Church and of so many of the ministry in neglecting or refusing to speak out and act promptly and efficiently on these great questions of reform. How could they more directly grieve and quench the Spirit of God than by such a course? Abandon the great work to which they are pledged and sworn, and yet profess to be Christians! No wonder that such a ministry should look coldly on revivals and find it impossible to promote them. After so much light has blazed before the churches on these subjects, it cannot be that they resist or neglect without great sin.

And shall it be persevered in? If so there can be no doubt that revivals must utterly cease—that the Spirit of God will be grieved entirely away from the ministry and the churches, and nothing better can be expected than utter and universal desolation.

Believe me, dear brethren, it grieves me greatly to feel constrained to speak thus. Is it not a shame; are we not ashamed and shall we not blush to see the Church of God not only turn back from reforming the world—refusing to lead in reform as she ought to do, and then turn round and oppose others who are compelled to lead for want of help and countenance of those who ought to go forward in these enterprises? If doctors of divinity—if ecclesiastical bodies, theological seminaries and colleges would but lead on in these enterprises, God forbid that they should not have their place. If they would but go forward the Church would follow them, and many who are now compelled to lead because these refuse, would rejoice to fall in behind and sustain them with all their might.

But if the church will not lead—if doctors of divinity, ecclesiastical bodies, colleges and seminaries will do nothing but get together to pass resolutions condemning the movements of reform, what shall be done? Shall they refuse to work in these departments and also hinder those who would work? Who pretends that so great wisdom has been manifested in the various branches of reform as might have been, had the spiritual leaders only taken the right position? What can be expected but error and confusion, while nearly all the spiritual influence in the world is brought to oppose instead of promote reforms? My brethren, if ecclesiastical bodies, colleges, and seminaries will only go forward—who will not bid them God speed? But if they will not go forward—if we hear little or nothing from them but complaint, denunciation, and rebuke in respect to almost every branch of reform, what can be done?

My soul is sick and agonized with such a state of things. The position of the Church is one of the greatest wonders of the world;—and yet we are gravely asking, why we do not have revivals of religion? Why has the Spirit of God forsaken us? and many are even glad to have revivals cease, and seem to be disposed to quell every thing down into a state of death-like apathy on every branch of reform.

Now until the Church shall arise and take a different attitude, I am confident that nothing else can be expected than a retrograde movement on the part of the Churches until not even a form of godliness remains among them.

Why cannot we all do in respect to reforms as Pres. Edwards did in respect to revivals? He fearlessly pointed out whatever was wrong and of evil tendency in the means used to promote them, and at the same time was careful to show a more excellent way. His opposition to what was wrong, although fearless and uncompromising, was never so prominent as to overshadow all his engagedness in promoting them. He was their powerful, zealous, and successful advocate and promoter. It became him then to speak out and rebuke whatever was wrong. Every body saw that his rebukes arose not from opposition to revivals as such, but to his great love for them and from a quenchless zeal to promote them. When he lifted his admonitory voice, the friends of revivals would listen because they knew it to be the voice of a friend and not an enemy of revivals. Everybody knew he spake of the evils sometimes connected with revivals because he loved them in their purity.

Now why cannot we all do so on the subject of reform? My brethren, let us all come forward and show ourselves to be reformers—put our heads and hearts together to promote every branch of reform and also revivals of religion, and then we shall hold a position in which we can successfully oppose and correct the errors of the day either in revivals or reforms. But who will listen to ministers, ecclesiastical bodies, doctors of divinity, missionary societies, or any body else who make no aggressive movements at all in respect to any reform and say almost nothing except to rebuke and condemn? They can talk eloquently of the evils incident to revivals, but are not like Pres. Edwards, zealous and successful in promoting them themselves. They can denounce the madness of abolitionists and the errors and extravagances of both the leaders and followers in other reforms; but alas, how few of them have any thing efficient or impressive to say to promote these great objects either by encouragement, instruction or counsel.

Now if ecclesiastical bodies generally, doctors of divinity, colleges and theological seminaries, had uniformly manifested zeal in all departments of reform, they would be heard. If ministers had manifested zeal and efficiency in these reforms, their churches would hear and respect them, and the ministry might lead them anywhere. But now the ministers are complaining that their churches are divided—that themselves are losing the confidence of their people—that ministerial influence is becoming paralyzed—and church influence an abomination.

Is it possible, my dearly beloved brethren, that we can remain blind to the tendencies of things—to the causes that are operating to produce alienation, division, distrust, to grieve away the Spirit, overthrow revivals, and cover the land with darkness and the shadow of death? Is it not time for us, brethren, to repent, to be candid and search out wherein we have been wrong and publicly and privately confess it, and pass public resolutions in our general ecclesiastical bodies, recanting and confessing what has been wrong—confessing in our pulpits, through the press, and in every proper way our sins as Christians and as ministers—our want of sympathy with Christ, our want of compassion for the slave, for the inebriate, for the wretched prostitute, and for all the miserable and ignorant of the earth.

May the Lord have mercy on us, my brethren.

Your brother, C. G. Finney

3 Theodore Weld:
Evangelical Reformer

American church historian William Warren Sweet has claimed that "perhaps the chief significance of Charles G. Finney lies not so much in the fact that he was the instrument in adding tens of thousands to the active ranks of the American churches, as in the circumstance that these new converts became active participants in every forward movement of their time."[1] To whichever fact one attributes Finney's "chief significance," his revivals certainly raised up an army of young converts who became the troops of the reform movements of his age. The antislavery forces in particular were drawn largely from the converts of Finney's revivals.

Probably the most important of these antislavery workers was Theodore Weld, converted under the ministry of Finney and for a while the evangelist's assistant. Weld devoted the whole of his life to reform and the antislavery struggle. According to the *Dictionary of American Biography*, "Weld was not only the greatest of the abolitionists; he was also one of the greatest figures of his time." Yet Weld was nearly lost to history, and it is only by a strange twist of events that we know as much about him as we do.

By natural modesty and firm convictions Weld resisted all efforts to thrust him into prominence. He declined the professorship of theology at Oberlin, insisting that it go to Finney, and the executive secretaryship of the American Anti-Slavery Society, arguing that his work was in the ranks. He refused invitations to speak at antislavery conventions because he "loathed"

1. William Warren Sweet, *Revivalism in America: Its Origin, Growth, and Decline* (New York: Charles Scribner's Sons, 1945), p. 160.

such "ostentatious display" and feared the "habit of gadding" from one convention to another. Weld would not let his speeches and letters be printed and published his books anonymously. He shunned the press and worked in the "West" (especially Ohio) away from the Eastern centers of influence. He chose, moreover, the obscurity of working in small towns "among the yeomanry," self-consciously arguing that "the great cities . . . must be burned down by *back fires*. The springs to touch . . . lie in the country."

Weld is consequently little represented in the sources historians use, and most interpretations of the antislavery movement focus on Boston and William Lloyd Garrison, editor of the *Liberator*. Such history naturally emphasizes liberal and Unitarian aspects of the movement and neglects the extent to which even Garrison was a product of revivalistic Evangelicalism. Garrison, moreover, was somewhat erratic and anticlerical and often more of a liability than an asset to the cause as it tried to permeate the Midwest and the church. Interpretations centering on Boston and Garrison, therefore, had difficulty explaining how antislavery sentiment became dominant throughout the North before the Civil War.

This New England and Garrisonian perspective was challenged in the 1930s by economist Gilbert Barnes of Ohio Wesleyan University who began to track down elusive references to Weld. Through Weld's grandson, Barnes finally located in an old farmhouse a trunk of letters that enabled him to offer a new interpretation of the abolitionist movement that emphasized its revivalistic origins. Barnes argued that "The agitation was accomplished not so much by heroes of reform as by very numerous obscure persons, prompted by an impulse religious in character and evangelical in spirit, which began in the Great Revival in 1830, was translated for a time into anti-slavery organization, and then broadened into a Congressional movement against slavery and the south."[2]

_____

2. Gilbert H. Barnes and Dwight L. Dumond, *Letters of Theodore Dwight Weld, Angelina Grimké Weld, and Sarah Grimké, 1822–1844* (Gloucester, Mass.: Peter Smith, 1965), vol. I, pp. xvi–xvii.

The validity of Barnes's thesis is still debated, but recent studies of abolitionism assume to great extent his perspective. The least that can be said is that revivalism (especially that of Finney) was a major force behind the pre–Civil War crusade against slavery. Barnes's work also brought to the fore a remarkable person all too long neglected: Theodore Weld, the greatest of the Evangelical abolitionists and reformers.

Weld was born in 1803 into a Connecticut minister's home that traced its ancestry through a long line of distinguished New England clergymen and theologians. A failure of eyesight during his studies at Phillips Academy caused Weld to drop out of school and take up lecturing on mnemonics—the art of memory improvement. After three years of astonishing success on the lecture platform (developing skills later to be put to other purposes) Weld returned to school at Hamilton College near Utica, New York.

Shortly thereafter Weld was called to Utica by the death of an uncle. Evangelist Charles G. Finney was in the area, and Weld's aunt tried to get her nephew to attend the revival meetings. Having already gained a reputation for ridiculing Finney, Weld declined, but finally agreed to attend a service at which another preacher was supposedly scheduled to speak. Once he was seated, his aunt and several other ladies filled up the pew. Weld attempted to leave when Finney arose to preach, but the ladies fell to their knees in prayer and pressed their heads against the pew in front blocking his only means of exit.

Theodore Weld resigned himself to his fate of listening to the evangelist. But Finney, tipped off in advance to Weld's presence, preached on the text, "one sinner destroyeth much good." Weld later reported that "for an hour, he just held me up on his toasting fork before that audience." Meeting Finney the next day in a store, Weld vented his disgust in "all the vocabulary of abuse the language afforded." Later ashamed of his actions, Weld sought out Finney to apologize, but before he could start, they embraced and fell to the floor, "sobbing and praying, sobbing and praying."

From this moment Weld was a disciple of Finney. He worked for a while in the "holy band" composed of Finney's assistants.

In that work Weld was a major force in pushing Finney toward one of his controversial "new measures"—that of allowing women to speak in "promiscuous" or mixed assemblies. This foreshadowed the later practice of women taking to the platform in defense of abolitionism and the consequent birth of feminism. A dozen years later Weld married one of the most prominent feminists and antislavery agitators of the era, Angelina Grimké. Weld claimed at that time that he had affirmed since he was a boy "that there is no reason why *woman* should not make laws, administer justice, sit in the chair of state, plead at the bar or in the pulpit, if she has the qualifications." Weld also broke the conventions of his day by suggesting that women should feel free to initiate courtship.

Weld soon moved into other reforms to which Finney's revivalism gave impetus. Under the influence of Charles Stuart, another member of Finney's "holy hand," Weld moved toward an antislavery position. He also regularly lectured on the question of temperance, marshaling for the cause a vast array of statistics and powerful rhetoric. In 1831 Weld became the general agent of the Society for Promoting Manual Labor in Literary Institutions. In this work he became an early advocate of a theme that permeated many institutions founded in the wake of Finney's revivals. This society encouraged several hours of manual labor each day, primarily out of concern for physical fitness, but the practice also permitted indigent students to earn their way through school. This was an early manifestation of a concern for total education and an antecedent of physical education.

But the antislavery struggle increasingly absorbed Weld's attention. At first he advocated colonization, but travels in the South and contacts with the emerging school of "immediate abolitionism" pushed him in a new direction. Weld urged his financial supporters in New York (primarily the Tappan brothers, see chap. 6) to join the antislavery struggle and to throw their resources behind it. These discussions climaxed in the founding in 1833 of the American Anti-Slavery Society. This organization then launched a major attack on colonization, and Finney himself signed the first letter of challenge to the Colonization Society demanding to know if they supported the "complete extinction of slavery in the United States."

In the midst of these discussions Weld enrolled in Lane Theological Seminary in Cincinnati and became embroiled in the abolitionist debates that led to the "Lane Rebellion" and the founding of Oberlin College. (These events are narrated in chap. 4). While in Cincinnati he spent every spare moment in the black community. In a survey of the three thousand blacks in Cincinnati, he discovered that more than three-fourths had recently bought their freedom and half still had members of their family in bondage. The suffering and grueling work to which these freedmen were subjected in attempting to scrape together funds to purchase the freedom of their relatives was more than Weld could stand. "After spending three or four hours, and getting facts, I was forced to stop from sheer heartache and agony."

Weld's identification with the black community was profound and belies the common accusation that abolitionists were nonetheless racially prejudiced.

If I ate in the City it was at their tables. If I slept in the City it was in their homes. If I attended parties, it was *theirs—weddings—theirs —Funerals—theirs—Religious meetings—theirs*—Sabbath schools—Bible Classes—theirs. During the 18 months that I spent at Lane seminary *I did not attend Dr. Beecher's Church once*. Nor did I attend any other of the Presbyterian Churches in the City except brother Mahan's, . . . I was with the colored people in their meetings by day and by night.

After leaving Lane, Weld accepted assignment as an agent for the newly founded American Anti-Slavery Society. In this work his experience and abilities found fullest expression. Testimonies left behind by his hearers indicate that he was a powerful and striking orator. Testifying to his "rare combination of talents," James G. Birney, also a prominent abolitionist, predicted, "I give him one year to abolitionize Ohio."

One key to Weld's impact was his adaption of the techniques of revivalism—especially the "protracted meeting" and the "call to decision"—to the antislavery cause. Weld would start by lecturing in the Presbyterian church in each town, but the first night's lecture would often incite a riot forcing him to seek other quarters. After a day or two, the resistance would break, and Weld would leave behind some new "converts" to found a local chapter of the American Anti-Slavery Society. Weld started his work in Ohio in October 1834. In May 1835, the national organization had 38 local chapters in Ohio (out of a total of 220). A year later the chapters totaled 527, but 133 were in Ohio.

Impressed with Weld's success, the national committee sent out seventy such agents as Jesus had sent out seventy disciples to preach. Weld and Henry B. Stanton, another Lane Rebel and later husband of feminist Elizabeth Cady Stanton, were called to New York to train this famous group of "Seventy"—over one-third of whom came out of the abolition struggle at Lane that Weld had ignited. By this means Weld multiplied his influence and played a major role in spreading the abolitionist gospel across the country.

Unfortunately Weld lost his voice about this time and retired from lecturing to work behind the scenes editing and writing. His first task was to produce in book form the "Bible Argument against Slavery" that he had developed and in the use of which he had instructed the Seventy. Though published anonymously, this book immediately went through several editions and became a major tool of the antislavery movement.

Soon after this, Weld first declared his long-concealed love for Angelina Grimké, one of the Seventy. This mutual affection, long sacrificed to the needs of the reform movement, now found culmination in an 1838 wedding. Committed to simplicity of life, the newly married couple had difficulty outfitting their home with furniture that was not "tricked out and covered with carved wood or bedizoned and gew gawed and gilded and tipt off with variegated colors." The wedding cake was prepared by a black confectioner who used nothing but "free sugar." ("Free sugar" was produced by freedmen rather than slaves—the economic boycott was freely used in the struggle against slavery.) The wedding ceremony was a simple exchange of vows in which Weld renounced the rights to Angelina's person and property granted him by the "sexist" laws of the age. Prayer was offered by both black and white clergymen. Soon thereafter Angelina was excommunicated by her Quaker society for marrying outside the sect.

Weld's next project was another book, *Slavery As It Is*. He combed Southern newspapers for evidence of the cruelty of slavery (such as ads seeking the return of runaway slaves identified by scars or other signs of mistreatment). These were compiled by Weld, Angelina, and her sister Sarah into a devastating critique of slavery that sold over one hundred thousand copies in the first year. This book was a major influence on Harriet Beecher Stowe, author of *Uncle Tom's Cabin*, who reported that she had been profoundly influenced by the debates on slavery Weld had initiated at Lane Seminary while her father had been president of the school. Mrs. Stowe claimed that she had slept with *Slavery As It Is* under her pillow while writing her novel.

Such research and propaganda prepared Weld for the next step in the struggle. In the early 1840s he was called to Washington to do research for John Quincy Adams who was leading the antislavery struggle in Congress. While in Washington Weld usually attended the churches of his black friends. Those services were noisier than he would have liked, but he much preferred them to the white churches in Washington whose religion seemed a sham put on for the sake of reputation and appearance.

Weld had become increasingly alienated from the churches of the era, and after leaving Washington he rejected the suggestion of Lewis Tappan that he take a church in New York City. Weld granted some exceptions, but his impression of the ministry from his years in the antislavery struggle was that

there is among the professed ministers of Christ such connivance at cherished sins, such truckling subserviency to power, such clinging with mendicant sycophancy to the skirts of wealth and influence, such humoring of pampered lusts, such cowering before bold transgression when it stalks among the high places of power with fashion in its train, or to sum up all, such floating in the wake of an unholy public sentiment, instead of beating back its waves with a "thus saith the Lord" and a "thou art the man"—that even men of the world who are shrewd discerners, regard them rather as the obsequious cooks and confectioners who cater for a capricious palate, than as the faithful physician who administers the medicine demanded by the disease, however much the patient may loathe it, and steadily pushes the probe to the core, whatever his struggles or upbraidings.

After service in Washington Weld retired to farming and teaching, though his work was often interrupted for antislavery activities, A superb teacher, he was entrusted with the children of many abolitionists who sought the particular mixture of modern techniques and moral education that Weld offered. Engaged in these and related activities, Weld lived to the age of ninety-one, dying in 1895.

The letters that Weld and the Grimké sisters left behind are a delight to read. Addressing themselves to issues that still bedevil the Evangelical world, these letters often offer startlingly pertinent advice.

They belie, for example, the common assumption that the abolitionists were concerned primarily with ridding themselves of complicity in the sin of slavery rather than the welfare of the slaves. They demonstrate that the Christian egalitarianism behind revivalist abolitionism understood the issues to be prejudice and caste as well as slavery. There was no sign of racial prejudice in Weld, who insisted that "persons are to be treated according to their intrinsic worth irrespective of Color, shape, condition, or what not." Weld's was a persistent voice calling the American Anti-Slavery Society to greater consistency. As Angelina wrote to Weld before their marriage: "I rejoice that you continue to identify yourself with our colored friends—to board with them, etc. I am sure that the poor and oppressed both *white* and black can never be benefitted without mingling with them on terms of equality."

This egalitarianism was carried over into their marriage, and Theodore and Angelina struggled continually with the problems of relating feminist convictions to their lives. Weld had been warned that a feminist like Angelina would be only "an obtrusive noisy clamorer" in the "domestic circle" and that it was "*impossible* for a man of high and pure feeling ever to *marry*" her—that "nature recoiled at it." Weld was convinced that "the devil of dominion over women will be one of the last that will be cast out" of men and worried about his ability to put his convictions into practice. But they were both convinced that their views freed them for a higher and deeper relationship that transcended the conventional patterns of male dominance and feminine wiles.

No one can doubt the profoundly Christian convictions that lay behind their lives. This is most poignant in love letters that reveal struggle with Christian commitment and its relationship to human commitments of love. Weld wondered to Angelina, "Do I love my blessed savior *less* because I *love you* as I do?" His own answer was that "My love for you has quickened me in love and gratitude . . . and in a more near and tender communion with him who loved us and died for us." In a similar way they were concerned that their marriage not hinder their effectiveness in the reforms to which they were committed—and to which they felt divinely called.

Something of the character of that Christian commitment is revealed in a very interesting sidelight. Their day, like our own, was troubled with arcane speculation about the end-times. Angelina, in particular, became agitated with the prophecies of William Miller whose predictions about the return of Christ placed the date in the midst of her pregnancy. Weld's response to Angelina was that

the study of prophecy has cast great witchery over minds of a certain cast. It powerfully stimulates curiosity, love of the marvellous, the element of superstition . . . the desire for novelty, etc. . . . I do not contend that prophecy is never to be studied, but that *God* is *first* to be studied, and so studied and communed with as to have the soul taken into captivity, moulded, filled with him; its principles, its taste, its tendencies, its habits, its intensities so incorporated with the mind of Christ . . . as to secure that subjection and allegiance and vital union with him which ushers into fullness of God.

Such convictions little prepare us for a later spiritual and theological struggle that led to a transformation of their faith. De-

spairing of the "profitless forms and dead formality and timid
time serving of the church and the ministry as a body," they
turned increasingly toward the "practicalities" of faith known
"experimentally." This involved moving from church forms and
doctrinal structures to a simple "loving and following Jesus"
that climaxed in Unitarianism.

What was involved in this pilgrimage is not entirely clear.
Weld's biographers have not given careful attention to this period and are not attuned to the questions we would ask. Weld
reflects a deeply biblical and committed faith pitted against the
churches of the time. He and Angelina shared the alienation of
the abolitionists during the 1840s as traditional churches refused to embrace reform. This disaffection was clearly related
to the revivalist alienation from the churches, and was therefore
"unorthodox" primarily in the sense that it failed to follow
patterns of traditional church life. How much more was involved is not certain. The letters exist for a study that not only
would illumine the pre–Civil War era but would also show how
the failure of the church to embrace the great moral concerns of
an age can drive out sensitive youth who will find moral leadership in other circles.

4 The Lane Rebellion and the Founding of Oberlin College

The major institution founded to perpetuate both the revivalism and the social positions of Charles G. Finney was Oberlin College. At Oberlin Jonathan Blanchard gave his address on the "State of the Perfect Society." Blanchard longed to teach at Oberlin, though he was unable to accept the invitation when it finally came. Many of today's Christian colleges were founded to be "little Oberlins." But Oberlin was not just another Christian college; it was hated in its time as a hotbed of radicalism. Socially, its major contribution was to the antislavery struggle. As Finney commented toward the end of the Civil War, "The fact is that Oberlin turned the scale in all of the Northwest." But Oberlin and its supporters also made major contributions to feminism, the peace movement, the doctrine of civil disobedience, temperance, and other reforms of the era.

It is difficult to know where to begin the story of Oberlin. Its prehistory is as fascinating as its history. One place to start is with Theodore Weld's decision to join the first class to enter Lane Theological Seminary in Cincinnati. Just as Weld was moving toward immediate abolitionism, this seminary was founded to reach the west with the spirit of revivalism and reform. Lyman Beecher, now somewhat reconciled to Finney and his ideals, had taken the presidency, in part at the urging of Finney. Beecher's brand of reform was more moderate and "polite." On the slavery issue he was committed to gradual abolition and colonization, but Lane did admit blacks (becoming one of the first institutions in America to drop the color line) and faced opposition for positions it did take.

Lane's first theological class consisted of about forty students. Of these, Theodore Weld was the only forthright abolitionist. One student later described "a general consent in the institution that slavery was somehow wrong and to be got rid of" but "not a readiness to pronounce it a sin." Part of Weld's motive in going to Lane was "to introduce anti-slavery sentiments, and have the whole subject thoroughly discussed." He succeeded.

Weld worked quietly to convert members of the campus colonization society to abolitionism. By the spring of 1834 he had convinced enough to challenge the rest to an eighteen-day debate on the two positions. At the conclusion the students voted almost unanimously in favor of immediate abolitionism and, following the dictates of sound strategy, they proceeded to organize an abolition society whose officers were all Southerners. Believing that "faith without works is dead," the students put their faith into practice by forming a "large and efficient organization for elevating the colored people of Cincinnati." This included literacy classes, lectures on academic subjects, Sunday schools, Bible classes, and research on the financial and social problems of Cincinnati's three thousand blacks. But most offensive was the students' insistence on treating blacks as social equals, eating in their homes, staying overnight with them, and even allowing themselves to be seen on the streets with young black women. This was too much for the townspeople who openly threatened mob action to get rid of the school. Beecher and the faculty warned the students of the dangerous consequences of "carrying the doctrine of intercourse into practical effect."

The board of trustees, mostly solid Cincinnati businessmen operating in the South, finally took action. In a special meeting called over the summer they insisted that "education must be completed before the young are fitted to engage in the collisions of active life," forbade even the discussion of such issues as slavery, and fired Professor John Morgan, the only faculty member who had sided with the students. A later meeting confirmed these actions arguing that "the location of the seminary . . . calls for some peculiar cautionary measures" for fear that the "prosperity of the Institution will be much retarded and its usefulness generally diminished." The *Cincinnati Journal* editorially supported the board with the comment that "a school, to prepare pious youth for preaching the gospel, has not legitimate place" for such concerns as abolitionism.

But for the students, the issue was moral integrity and principle. They raised the matter of freedom of speech, declaring that "free discussion being a duty is consequently a right, and as such, is inherent and inalienable." At least forty students withdrew from the school in protest. Most of these moved across town and set up an informal "free seminary" at which they instructed themselves in theology and continued their work among the blacks of Cincinnati.

Meanwhile, in another part of Ohio, another project was developing—also deeply influenced by Finney. John J. Shipherd and Philo P. Stewart were founding a colony and a school, Christian in character and abolitionist in conviction. Those who joined this community pledged themselves to a particular lifestyle expressive of their understanding of the Christian faith. The "Oberlin Covenant" contains twelve items, but since it epitomizes the self-understanding of Oberlin and contains so many themes echoed in current discussions, it is reproduced here in its entirety:

1. Providence permitting, we engage as soon as practicable to remove to the Oberlin Colony, in Russia, Lorain County, Ohio, and there to fix our residence, for the express purpose of glorifying God in doing good to men to the extent of our ability.

2. We will hold and manage our estates personally, but pledge as perfect a community of interest as though we held a community of property.

3. We will hold in possession no more property than we believe that we can profitably manage for God, as His faithful stewards.

4. We will, by industry, economy, and Christian self-denial, obtain as much as we can, above our necessary personal or family expenses, and faithfully appropriate the same for the spread of the Gospel.

5. That we may have time and health for the Lord's service, we will eat only plain and wholesome food, renouncing all bad habits, and especially the smoking and chewing of tobacco, unless it is

necessary as a medicine, and deny ourselves all strong and unnecessary drinks, even tea and coffee, as far as practicable, and everything expensive, that is simply calculated to gratify the palate.

6. That we may add to our time and health money for the service of the Lord, we renounce all the world's expensive and unwholesome fashions of dress, particularly tight dressing and ornamental attire.

7. And yet more to increase our means of serving Him who bought us with His blood, we will observe plainness and durability in the construction of our houses, furniture, carriages, and all that appertains to us.

8. We will strive continually to show that we, as the body of Christ, are members one of another; and will, while living, provide for the widows, orphans, and families of the sick and needy, as for ourselves.

9. We will take special pains to educate our children thoroughly, and to train them up, in body, intellect, and heart, for the service of the Lord.

10. We will feel that the interests of the Oberlin Institute are identified with ours, and do what we can to extend its influence to our fallen race.

11. We will make special efforts to sustain the institutions of the gospel at home and among our neighbors.

12. We will strive to maintain deep-toned and elevated personal piety, to "provoke each other to love and good works," to live together in all things as brethren, and to glorify God in our bodies and spirits, which are His.

But by 1834 Oberlin Institute was in desperate financial straits, and Shipherd was sent East to look for funds and a president for the struggling school. One report indicates that in a preparatory session of prayer and fasting Shipherd received the definite, but inexplicable, impression that he should go East by way of Cincinnati! There he visited Asa Mahan, the major defender of the Lane students among the members of Lane's board of trustees. (Mahan was pastor of the only Presbyterian church in the city that Weld had found interested in the slaves and blacks and the same church that Jonathan Blanchard was later to pastor.) Immediately there opened up the opportunity to gain for Oberlin a new president (Asa Mahan), an outstanding and popular faculty member (John Morgan—fired for his identification with the Lane Rebels), a sizable theological department of mature students, as well as the financial backing of Arthur Tappan, the New York businessman providing funds for the "free seminary."

But Mahan, Morgan, and the Lane Rebels would come only on condition that absolute freedom of speech be guaranteed on all reform issues and that blacks be admitted with whites. Shaken by the events at Lane, Oberlin trustees were at first reluctant but finally accepted a compromise. Finney agreed to come as professor of theology if the trustees would leave the matter of the admission of blacks in the hands of the faculty. With Mahan, Morgan, and Finney on the faculty, that decision was never in question. This compromise permitted the confluence of the radical abolitionism of the Lane Rebels and the communitarian and life-style oriented radicalism of the Oberlin Colony. The foundations were laid for the emergence of the distinctive Christian radicalism of Oberlin College.

By the time the new school was announced, Oberlin had become the last refuge for radical students. All over the country conservative interests had suppressed antislavery societies and purged campuses of abolitionists. Nearly three hundred students poured into Oberlin the first year, and more the next—many more than Oberlin could physically accommodate. Immediately, too, opposition surfaced. One observer insisted that "Oberlin had before enemies enough for one Semny. Now they will increase ten fold." And Shipherd discovered that "Finneyism, Abolitionism, *etc.* are excuses of multitudes for not giving funds." But Shipherd and Oberlin believed that "public Institutions no less than private Christians must do right however contrary to popular sentiment." On this great principle Oberlin College was launched.

"Oberlinism" was a complex ideology. The institution was first and foremost a Christian college. Finney insisted that Oberlin "make the conversion of sinners and the sanctification of Christians the paramount work and subordinate to this all the educational operations." College life was intensely religious with frequent periods of revival. Students and faculty alike regularly conducted revival meetings during vacations. Missions was also a dominant concern. By 1836 the campus had six different missionary societies, and in 1838 this missionary impulse began to focus on the American Indian. (Oberlin was concerned with more than missions to the Indian and opposed government efforts at relocation and other violations of treaties.)

But Oberlin would have nothing to do with Christian faith unrelated to reform and boasted that "Oberlin College has been greatly successful in making her students intelligent and vigorous reformers." President Mahan insisted that "the fundamental spirit and aim of Christianity is the correction of all abuses, a universal conformity to the laws of our own existence as far as revealed to the mind, and a quenchless thirst for knowledge on all subjects pertaining to the duties and interest of humanity." At the same time Oberlin prided itself on hearing all sides of any issue, avoiding personal denunciation in a spirit of love for the oppressor as well as the oppressed, and maintaining a stance of "universal reform" rather than "fanatical" or "ultraistic" commitment to a single cause.

Oberlin's great issue was the antislavery struggle. Soon after the students arrived, they founded the Oberlin Anti-Slavery Society whose two hundred members pledged to work for the "immediate emancipation of the whole colored race." Oberlin provided at least sixteen of the famous Seventy sent out as agents of the American Anti-Slavery Society (and more were Lane Rebels who did not move on to Oberlin). As was common in such work, these lecturers and organizers endured mob violence and other forms of abuse. Oberlinites were prominent in state and national antislavery organizations. Sermons and lectures on campus regularly returned to this theme. Convictions were so strong that residents of Oberlin found July 4 a "cruel mockery" (since it celebrated only the freedom of the white race) and preferred instead to honor August 1 (the anniversary of emancipation in the British West Indies). Nor did such concerns stop upon graduation. Oberlin alumni fanned out over the country to work among members of the black race, especially by founding schools.

Oberlin wished to make the whole Christian church an "antislavery society." The means was "moral suasion" or the use of

Finney's "new measure revival techniques." The Oberlin Church passed a resolution that "as Slavery is a Sin no person shall be invited to preach or Minister to this church, or any Br. be invited to commune who is a slaveholder." The wider Congregational association of which Oberlin was a part declared that "*oppression* in all its forms is sin" and vowed to have "no Christian communion with those who practice slavery, nor with any who justify the system." When church agencies, such as missionary societies, refused to make abolitionism a firm plank in their policy statements, Oberlinites worked for the establishing of separate antislavery mission boards.

The peace movement also found support at Oberlin. Here, though, opinion was not uniform. First into the fray in 1840 was the Oberlin Non-Resistance Society that renounced all use of force. More typical was the Oberlin Peace Society founded in 1843. This group allowed that war might in some cases be just—though it took several weeks of debate to establish this position. But this conclusion was not used to avoid intense peace activity through writing, lecturing, education, and conferences. Nor did Oberlin hesitate to dissent from American war policy. The *Oberlin Evangelist* attacked President Polk for risking war with Britain through his "expansionist" policy of demanding all of the Oregon territory. The Mexican War provoked this response: "Wars of aggression like this we not only deprecate and deplore, but most unqualifiedly condemn. The conscience of the world and the court of heaven are against us." A year later the same war was described as "most dishonorable, unjust, and nefarious . . . conceived in sin."

Oberlin also made contributions to the women's movement, though it resisted the style of the "woman's rights" crusade. It was the first coeducational college in the world, a step that met much resistance. (Even reformer Lyman Beecher said that "this amalgamation of the sexes won't do. If you live in a Powder House, you blow up once in a while.") But opinion divided on whether women should speak in public, even though Finney's revival techniques had helped open up this possibility. Mahan supported the women (especially as his own daughter neared the time of her "commencement essay") but was not able to carry the rest of the faculty. Antoinette Brown, the first woman to be ordained, was only permitted to attend theological lectures "unofficially." But she did attend and completed a theological education. The education Oberlin provided for women laid the foundation for their progressing even further into the women's rights movement. As a result Oberlin graduated many feminists of the era. Among these were Lucy Stone (whose name became notorious as the household expression for a woman who kept her family name in marriage) and Betsy Cowles (president of the Second National Women's Rights Convention).

An interesting sidelight in this story is Oberlin's commitment to "physiological reform." The institution was deeply influenced by the philosophy of the manual labor schools that Theodore Weld had worked to propogate. Students usually had four hours of manual labor daily—to support themselves, to preserve appreciation for physical labor, but primarily for the sake of health. Oberlin was deeply permeated by the health food movement of that time. Shipherd, Stewart, Mahan, Weld, and Finney were all disciples of Sylvester Graham, inventor of the "Graham Cracker." Graham taught not only total abstinence from alcoholic beverages, but also from "tobacco, tea, coffee, and all other stimulants," as well as "pepper, mustard, oil, vinegar, etc." Oberlinites tended to be vegetarian, and almost all sweets were outlawed.

Oberlin was also in the vanguard of educational reform. Shipherd had consulted educational reformers in developing plans for the new school. Oberlin prepared teachers for the new "common schools" for the masses. (Horace Mann had effected the founding of the first state-supported "normal school" only in 1839.) In the 1840s innovative new courses in teaching methods were developed. This was not taught in the more traditional schools. Oberlinites advocated a form of "progressive education" that governed by "moral principles, instead of the rod and the rule." Some have credited Oberlin with introducing the study of music to American education. Finney himself was quite musical (he sang, directed choirs, and played the bass viol) and refused to teach at Oberlin unless the first faculty included a professor of music. Oberlin also pioneered in business and agricultural education.

Oberlin was politically committed to the progressive movements of the period. Early members of Oberlin Colony had been conservative Whigs, but antislavery sentiments pushed them in another direction—toward the Liberty party, an abolitionist third party, and later into the new, antislavery Republican party. In 1856 the *Oberlin Evangelist* called for support for "Free Press, Free Speech, Free Men, Fremont and Victory." In most elections the Oberlin Colony voted solidly Republican. This political persuasion put them at odds with the surrounding Democratic political establishment and gave a political cast to Oberlin's commitment to reform.

But the really explosive issue that rocked Oberlin and for which she gained particular notoriety was the civil disobedience she advocated. This doctrine developed gradually as Oberlin supported the underground railroad by which slaves were smuggled through the North to freedom in Canada. This activity climaxed in a court case that played a major role in the development of American civil liberties. But that story deserves separate attention.

It is difficult to overstate the extent to which Oberlin identified
with the black and the slave—or the extent to which this fact
generated opposition to Oberlin's course. When it was announced that students would be admitted irrespective of sex or
color, Oberlin's financial agent in New England wrote back that
his area would scarcely accept coeducation and that everything
possible must be done to avoid the accusation of "amalgamation of the races." He feared that "as soon as your *darkies* begin
to come in . . . the whites will begin to leave—and at length
your Institute will change colour." Unless this policy were
dropped, he warned, the school would "be blown *sky high* and
you will have a black establishment there *thro' out*."

Humorist Artemas Ward amused his readers in 1865 by writing that Oberlin was "a very good college" though it was his
"onbiassed 'pinion that they go it rather too strong on Ethi-
opians." His description of the streets in Oberlin had wide
circulation. "As a faithful historian, I must menshum the fack
that on rainy dase white people can't find their way threw the
streets without the gas is lit, ther bein such a numerosity of
cullerd pussons in the town."

There was apparently no bar at Oberlin to social intercourse
between the races. Black students boarded and roomed with
whites. The Ladies' Principal reported in 1866 that the black
women "have been seated at different tables by the side of white
ladies, and if it so happened opposite white young men." In the
1840s one young male student wrote home that "about every
fifth one at the table is a darky" and added that "the best
appearing chap I have seen here is black." Artemas Ward no
doubt exaggerated in saying that "at the Boarding House the

cullured people sit at the first table. What they leave is maid into hash for the white people." But all of this appeared so shocking to the outside that one student had to write home that "we dont have to kiss the Niggars nor speak to them without we are to mind to." But it should be added, that while there seem to have been no cases of interracial marriage, there was no special bar to social intercourse of the opposite sexes—and even some reports of romances.

Oberlin, however, struggled with how far to go in identification with the black race, particularly when their concerns pushed them to the edge of legality. The underground railroad especially raised these issues. The college was one of the most important "stations," and hundreds of escaped slaves passed through Oberlin.

The college maintained a Fund for Fugitives, and expenses were often paid out of public funds. Very often faculty homes (even the president's) were used to house escaped slaves. Those who died in Oberlin were buried at public expense in the village cemetery. The town prided itself on never having lost a single "passenger." This was not an easy record to maintain. As early as 1841 Oberlinites were forced to recapture escaped slaves seized by authorities.

All of this ran directly counter to the federal fugitive slave laws that required the return of escaped slaves. Such laws had been on the books since 1793, but the 1830s and 1840s saw efforts to tighten up such laws on both the national and the state level. Oberlin's response to this was based on a doctrine of civil disobedience that appealed to "higher" or "divine law." Evangelist Finney himself made major contributions to the development of this doctrine. Historian Charles Cole has called this "one of his chief contributions to the cause" of abolitionism.[1]

In 1839 the Ohio legislature overwhelmingly adopted a statute that in effect extended over all of Ohio the jurisdiction of Kentucky with regard to fugitive slaves. One Oberlin professor had to go into hiding after helping one old black woman to

1. Charles C. Cole, Jr., *The Social Ideas of the Northern Evangelists 1826–1860* (New York: Columbia University Press, 1954), p. 208.

escape. Finney himself introduced a resolution into the next meeting of the Ohio Anti-Slavery Society declaring that such a statute was not "obligatory upon the citizens of this State, inasmuch as its requisitions are a palpable violation of the Constitution of this State, and of the United States, of the common law and of the law of God." The rationale for this affirmation of civil disobedience was spelled out:

Resolved, That for the following obvious reasons, we regard it, as a well settled principle of both common and constitutional law, that no human legislation can annul, or set aside the law or authority of God.

a. The most able writers on elementary law, have laid it down as a first principle, that whatever is contrary to the law of God, is not law.

b. Where a bond, or other written instrument, or anything else, is of immoral tendency, courts of law have refused to recognize it as legal and obligatory.

c. The administration of oaths, or affirmations, in courts of justice, is a recognition of the existence and supreme authority of God.

d. The Constitution of this State expressly recognizes the axiom, that no human enactment can bend the conscience, or set aside our obligations to God.

e. The general instrument of which the federal Government is founded, recognizes the same truth—that rights conferred by our Creator as inalienable, can never be cancelled, or set aside by human enactments.

f. The administration of oaths, or affirmations in all departments of the general and state governments, is a recognition of the truth, that God's authority is supreme.

Finney's convictions, if anything, grew stronger over the years. Oberlin was particularly offended by the federal Fugitive Slave Law of 1850. Finney called it the "Fugitive Slave Bill" even after it was passed, arguing that nothing so opposed to the divine will and the United States Constitution should ever be called a law. He wrote such convictions into his *Lectures on Systematic Theology*, insisting that "no human constitution or enactment can, by any possibility, be law that recognizes the right of one human being to enslave another." Finney argued that "We are bound in all cases to disobey, when human legislation contravenes moral law, or invades the rights of conscience."

The whole campus was embroiled in these issues. During the 1850s the literary societies debated such propositions as "Ought Christians to obey the new Fugitive Law?" "Ought a functionary of the government either to execute a law which in his opinion conflicts with the divine law or else resign his office?" "Ought we to resist by violence the execution of the Fugitive Slave Law?" and "Does the injustice of a law free the citizens of the U.S. from the moral obligation to obey it?"

Students (and faculty) engaged in civil disobedience, not only in the underground railroad and by recapturing escaped slaves seized by the authorities, but also in some cases by invading the South to free slaves. George Thompson served five years in a Missouri penitentiary for trying to help two slaves escape to Illinois. Calvin Fairbank claimed to have liberated forty-seven slaves but served two prison terms of four and twelve years for such activities. The climax of these efforts was the notorious "Oberlin-Wellington Rescue Case" that gained for Oberlin a world-wide reputation.

In early 1858 John Price, a fugitive slave, sought refuge in Oberlin. That summer four armed men from the South paid a teen-ager to lure John out of town, ostensibly to help dig up some potatoes. Once outside of Oberlin, John was seized and taken to nearby Wellington to await the next train. Fortunately Oberlinites returning to town met the fleeing party on its way to Wellington and divined what had happened. By ringing the chapel bell, they alerted the colony, and a crowd of several hundred gathered in Wellington. The situation presented a conflict of values for the largely nonviolent Oberlinites, but after some hesitation the hotel was stormed, and John was rescued without, in the words of one narrator, "so much as bruising a finger." John was rushed back to Oberlin and hidden in the home of J. H. Fairchild (professor of moral and mental philosophy and Finney's successor as president) before being spirited off to Canada.

Such a flagrant challenge to federal authority could not remain unpunished. For the local Democratic establishment, it provided a chance to "get" Republican Oberlin, to strike a major blow at the underground railroad, and to demonstrate a willingness to enforce the unpopular fugitive slave laws. Indictments were brought against twenty-one identifiable citizens of Oberlin as well as against some residents of Wellington (though these were not pressed so that the trial could focus exclusively on Oberlin and play on the local resentment of Oberlinism). Among the Oberlinites indicted were Henry E. Peck, associate professor of mental and moral philosophy (Oberlin's professor of Christian ethics), and James M. Fitch, Oberlin's Sunday school superintendent. The trial opened on April 5, 1859, and quickly degenerated into a political struggle (jury, judge, and prosecutors were all Democrats ideologically opposed to Oberlin) and a propaganda battle whose volleys were heard around the world.

The district attorney portrayed the Oberlinites as revolutionaries, characterized the "higher law" as the "Devil's law," and claimed that "Higher Law people ran into the predicament of free love and infidelity." He advised the Oberlinites to preach "the Bible and not politics." Replying to accusations that their actions were unpatriotic, Peck denied that "there is no patriotism where there is not an acknowledgment of the maxim, 'Our country right or wrong,' " and insisted that he was a follower of a "higher patriotism" that sought to keep the country honest and true to its highest ideals and revolutionary convictions. The Oberlin defense explicitly advocated the doctrine of a divine or "higher law" but rested most of its case on such issues as the questionable identification of John and the constitutionality of the Fugitive Slave Law.

But unavoidably some of the argument focused on the question of the "higher law." Peck insisted that "We must obey God always, and human law, social and civil, when we can." This "Divine Will was well expounded in the life of Christ" whose gospel was such that "those who should follow Him, should minister to the needy; that the poor and forlorn would be blessed by it; that those 'sick and in prison' would be cheered by it; and that it would strike the iron from countless wretches unjustly bound."

The Oberlin prisoners did manage several astute propaganda coups. (Their imprisonment was in part because they refused to post bail to dramatize the fact they were in jail for their convictions.) Urgent appeals to the state and federal courts were unsuccessful but did publicize the case. Money poured into the defense fund from around the world. The prisoners used their confinement to create the aura of martyrdom. They published a paper from their jail in Cleveland. (Fortunately their jailer was antislavery in conviction and sympathetic to their cause!) This paper, entitled *The Rescuer*, expounded "the nature and claims of the Higher Law, the iniquities of American slavery, and the injustice and illegality of the Fugitive Slave Act." But perhaps the greatest coup on behalf of the prisoners was bringing four hundred "Sabbath school children" to march through the streets of Cleveland with banners before visiting the jail to have services with their imprisoned Sunday School superintendent James M. Fitch. Ethics professor Peck was allowed to preach to crowds gathered in the jailyard.

But political power still reigned, and it looked as if the Oberlinites would be convicted until someone came up with the ploy of arresting the four "slave-catchers" and bringing them to trial in Oberlin for kidnapping. In Oberlin the judge, jury, and prosecutors would all be Republican, operating on a different interpretation of the constitutionality of the Fugitive Slave Law. Conviction was certain, and the trial would prevent the major witnesses in the government's case from appearing in the Cleveland court. Just to be sure that their prisoners were not released before the trial, the sheriff on whom the papers would have to be served left town for several days. The situation was finally resolved by dropping both sets of charges and releasing both sets of prisoners. The Oberlinites returned triumphantly to Oberlin to celebrate their victory while the Cleveland *Plain Dealer* bitterly complained that "the government has been beaten at last with law, Justice, and facts all on its side, and Oberlin, with its rebellious high law creed, is triumphant."

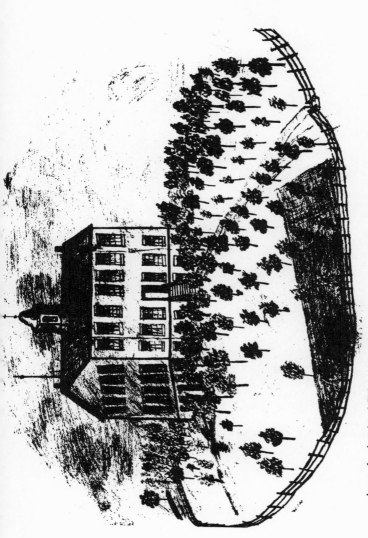

An early sketch of Illinois Institute showing the building that is now the center section of Blanchard Hall, named for the first two presidents of Wheaton College. (*Courtesy of Wheaton College Archives*)

Jonathan Blanchard, first president of Wheaton College.

Evangelist Charles Grandison Finney.

Tent used by Charles G. Finney for his "protracted" revival meetings when other accommodations were not available. Seating up to three thousand persons, this tent was often used for Oberlin College commencements and later for American Anti-Slavery Society rallies.

Reformer Theodore Weld.

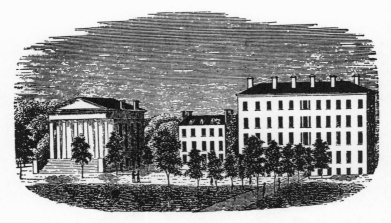

Lane Theological Seminary, Cincinnati, Ohio, the site of the "Lane Rebellion" of abolitionist students.

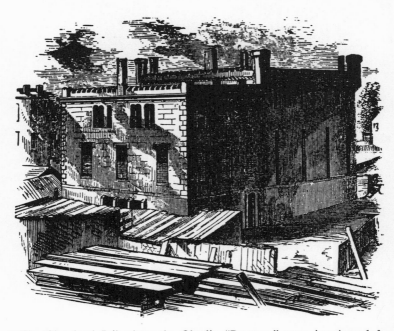

The Cleveland Jail where the Oberlin "Rescuers" were imprisoned for disobeying the Fugitive Slave Law.

Asa Mahan, first president of Oberlin College.

CELEBRATION

BY THE

DISFRANCHISED AMERICANS

OF

OBERLIN, OHIO,
FIRST OF AUGUST, 1846.

William H. Day, Northampton, Mass., President.
Daniel Peales, Lexington, Ky., V. P.

ORDER OF EXERCISES.

MUSIC.
PRAYER.
MUSIC.

1. **Freedom's Dawn.**—AN ORATION.
   ALLEN M. BLAND, *Charleston, S. C.*

2. **The Duty of American Women relative to American Slavery.**—AN ESSAY.
   MISS EMELINE M. CROOKER, *Troy, N. Y.*

3. **Emancipation in the West Indies---Slavery in the United States.**—AN ORATION.
   SAMUEL GRAY, *Columbia, Tenn.*

MUSIC.

4. **Liberty and Slavery contrasted.**—AN ORATION.
   FIELDING SMITHEA, *Philadelphia, Pa.*

5. **Ought these things so to be?**—AN ESSAY.
   MISS MARY H. CRABB, *Oberlin.*

6. **The Bondman's Appeal.**—AN ORATION.
   THEODORIC A. WALKER, *Petersburg, Va.*

MUSIC.

7. **Results of Emancipation.**—AN ORATION.
   CHARLES M. WILSON, *Cincinnati.*

8. **Why do we rejoice to day?**—AN ESSAY.
   MISS LUCY STONE, *West Brookfield, Mass.*

MUSIC.

9. **Human Brotherhood.**—AN ORATION.
   JAMES MONROE, *Canterbury, Ct.*

MUSIC.

Program for the celebration of August 1. Oberlin identification with the slaves forced many to honor this date, upon which the slaves in the West Indies were emancipated, rather than July 4, because the latter celebrated only the freedom of white Americans. *(Courtesy of Oberlin College)*

Businessman Arthur Tappan.

Businessman Lewis Tappan.

The Oberlin-Wellington Rescue Case, however, proved to be a major force for raising consciousness on the issue of slavery. One historian of Oberlin has ranked the episode with the publication of *Uncle Tom's Cabin* and John Brown's raid on Harper's Ferry as events that stirred the public imagination before the Civil War. William Lloyd Garrison wrote his greetings in these words: "What a humiliating spectacle is presented to the world in the trials now going on at Cleveland of your humane and Christian citizens who so nobly delivered the spoiled out of the hands of the oppressor! . . . But this very persecution will give a fresh impetus to our noble cause." And so it did. But the importance of the Oberlin-Wellington Rescue Case is not confined to its impact in that period on the awareness of the slavery problem. A record of the case has been recently reprinted as a landmark in the development of American civil liberties.

The experiences of the Oberlinites in this case pushed them even closer to a position that can only be called revolutionary. During the trial the Oberlin students began to debate such questions as "Resolved that it is the duty of the citizens of Oberlin to forcibly resist the Fugitive Slave Law, henceforth and forever." They also began to consider whether the Oberlin prisoners should be released by force. One defense lawyer argued for "the right of revolution, the ultimate and legitimate resort of people who find their governments too oppressive longer to be borne." In this the Oberlinites appealed to the precedent of American revolutionary origins. As one of the prisoners put it:

We belong to no "modern school" of politics or theology, and lay claim to no new light on these subjects. We belong to the school of the Fathers, who having been driven from their native land by the persecutions of their government, taught their children that "resistance to tyrants is obedience to God"; or to the more ancient school, which exclaimed to the existing authorities, "Whether it be right to hearken unto you more than unto God, judge ye"; or to that still more ancient, which said to the king, "We will not serve thy Gods nor worship the golden image which thou hast set up."

Such teachings enabled Oberlin to sympathize with John Brown, who had been preparing for his raid on Harper's Ferry

during the Oberlin-Wellington Rescue Trial. Two Oberlin
blacks, harness-maker Lewis Sheridan Leary and student John
A. Copeland, died in that episode. Leary was killed during the
raid, and Copeland was executed a few days later. The chapel
bell tolled for an hour on the day of Brown's execution. The
student paper reported that in a memorial service "Professor
Peck surpassed himself. . . . His summer's incarceration has
given him a rich experience from which to draw, when about to
speak for the downtrodden, or account the deeds of the martyrs
of liberty." A member of the board of trustees declared in a
funeral sermon that "we can see no signs of hallucination or of
infatuation in John Brown. We esteem him as one of the Wise
Men of our times." At a joint meeting of the men's literary
societies, one toast to John Brown was in these words: "to John
Brown: the hero of Harper's Ferry—the true representative of
the American idea!"

Arthur and Lewis Tappan:
The Businessman As Reformer

Contemporary stereotypes are shaken by the realization that the
major financial backing and organizational leadership behind
the abolitionist crusade derived from the man who founded Dun
and Bradstreet (the Wall Street credit rating firm) and his silk-
merchant brother. Lewis and Arthur Tappan were two of the
most prominent and wealthy businessmen in pre–Civil War
New York. Yet these two men so threw themselves into the
reform movements of the era that one tribute after Arthur's
death affirmed that "in the slavery agitation, its beginning, its
extent, its power, its results, it may be said, without a question,
that Arthur Tappan was the pivotal centre of the whole movement."

The Tappan brothers were born in the late 1780s into a large
and pious family in Northampton, Massachusetts. The Tappans
lived there for a time in the old house of Jonathan Edwards—
not inappropriately, in view of the deep Edwardsean piety that
permeated the home under the influence of their mother, Sarah
Tappan. Later, as apprenticed clerks in Boston, the brothers sat
for a while under the preaching of Unitarian William Ellery
Channing. Lewis at first embraced Unitarianism, serving in
1825 as treasurer of the American Unitarian Association. But
in 1828 he returned to Evangelicalism, explaining his action
publicly in a *Letter from a Gentleman in Boston to a Unitarian
Clergyman of that City*.

In New York the Tappan brothers later became the major
financial supporters of evangelist Charles G. Finney, funding
many of his pet projects. Lewis and Arthur Tappan were consistent advocates and practitioners of a form of Evangelical
religion that, like the Evangelical Revival of the preceding cen-

tury, found a positive role theologically for "good works." Lewis described the faith of his brother: "With a firm belief in the evangelical faith, he relied upon the mercy of God through the atoning sacrifice of the Saviour, discarding all thoughts of his good deeds as meriting reward in another life, although he firmly believed that as evidences of piety they were essential."

It is difficult to overestimate the impact of the Tappans upon both the business community and the reform movements. Their fortunes were made in Arthur's silk company (the largest silk jobber in the country) where their success was a result of absolute honesty, a preference for "cash sales," and a new system of "fixed prices." The Tappans pioneered in fixed prices for all customers instead of haggling and deals. Customers knew what to expect, and strangers could trust them. By the high-volume and low-mark-up formula of a modern K-Mart, the Tappans grew rich, grossing over a million dollars a year.

Their business survived a devastating fire only to go under in the financial collapse of 1837. Arthur Tappan suspended payments owing more than a million dollars, but within eighteen months he was back on his feet, having paid all his obligations with interest. Arthur was also the founder of the *Journal of Commerce* in 1827, a new daily to "exert a wholesome moral influence" by "abstaining particularly from publishing immoral advertisements" for such things as "spiritous liquors, circuses, and theatres."

Lewis Tappan set out on his own in 1841 by founding the Mercantile Agency (the antecedent of today's Dun and Bradstreet). This company set up a network of contacts throughout the country to provide credit ratings for businessmen. In an increasingly mobile and widespread economy this new idea helped provide stability when personal knowledge of businessmen was no longer available by enquiry around the local community.

In spite of such wealth the Tappan brothers preferred to live unostentatiously, considering themselves stewards of the money God had given them. Lewis Tappan authored late in his life a pamphlet entitled *Is It Right to Be Rich?* (1869), answering the question largely in the negative in an effort to combat a less "responsible" postwar pattern of the accumulation of wealth. All of their lives the Tappans plowed most of their wealth back into various philanthropies, benevolent societies, and social reform movements.

Arthur Tappan especially made major contributions to these groups and served many as officer or board member. With an anonymous gift to the American Bible Society he hoped "to supply every family in the United States with a Bible." He supported the American Sunday School Union, encouraging it to "have a Sabbath School formed within two years in every town" in the newly settled Mississippi Valley. His contributions to the American Tract Society went for presses and printing of materials—he wanted to "give two tracts to every family in the valley of the Mississippi." Tappan also attempted to fight prostitution and rescue its practitioners by founding a Magdalen Society modeled after a British counterpart. But an 1831 report of the society was so explicit and devastating that public reaction forced him to back off from this project.

The Tappan brothers were a little severe and humorless, given to a scrupulosity that sometimes annoyed their colleagues —even those also devoted to the same benevolent enterprises. They were committed to the Temperance Movement, and Arthur led the campaign to replace communion wine with a "nonalcoholic burgundy" that he had especially imported from France—a cause much mocked in the New York press. He was also active in the General Union for Promoting the Observance of the Christian Sabbath. In this work he opposed laws requiring postal clerks to work on Sunday, supported the founding of a new six-day stage line so that Christians would not have to patronize those that operated on Sunday, advocated boycotting products made on Sunday, and so on. But what really annoyed some ministers was his questioning whether churches should allow themselves the luxury of being lit with gas from companies using Sunday labor. Arthur was not at all amused when a churchman questioned whether silk goods were immoral since they were luxury items produced by silkworms that worked on Sunday.

But more significant was Tappan support for the "free

church" movement in New York City. This little-known aspect of American church history was a protest against selling and renting pews to support the construction and maintenance of church buildings. (For more on this movement, see chap. 9.) Opponents of this practice argued that the result was the exclusion (or at least embarrassment) of the poor and a seating pattern according to wealth that could not be squared with biblical teachings against "being a respector of persons" or giving preference to wealth and status. Such sentiments led a number of Presbyterian ministers to found in 1830 in New York City a "Third Presbytery" consisting of "free churches" where pews were open to all regardless of class or wealth. Within two years these missions boasted a membership of nearly four thousand.

The Tappan brothers put up much of the money for these churches. The second of six such churches founded was a remodeled theater called the Chatham Street Chapel. This church had been prepared especially for evangelist Charles G. Finney when the Tappans finally convinced him to take a settled pastorate in New York City after his revivals in the West and upstate New York. The pastors of the "free churches" were all practitioners of Finney's "new measure" revivalism, and the congregations consisted largely of converts from Finney's campaigns. These churches were closely identified with the reform movements, providing finances, hosting abolitionist conventions and other rallies, and producing the troops of the movements.

The extent of Lewis Tappan's commitment to the egalitarianism implicit in the "free church" movement can be judged from one of his disagreements with the church. Lewis Tappan wrote in one letter that "some of us thought that the 'negro Pew' should be done away—for although people were invited to sit where they pleased, it was understood, by whites and blacks, that the colored people should sit by themselves in a certain place in the galleries. . . . In the Chatham St. Chapel we succeeded in bringing the colored part of the congregation downstairs to occupy a range of slips on one side of the church, but were never able, though Mr. Finney was the pastor, to abolish the distinction altogether, in seats, and allow the people to sit, in fact, as they were invited to, wherever they chose. . . . Finding nothing could be done in a matter so near to my heart I left the church."

Such concerns found a major outlet in the abolitionist struggles. This reform increasingly absorbed the time and wealth of the Tappan brothers. They had long been concerned about the slavery issue in a general way. They supported for a time the American Colonization Society—though in part it must be admitted because of their interest in opening up new areas of trade among the freed slaves attempting to establish Liberia. But the Tappans gradually withdrew from this movement. Arthur disapproved of the rum trade that had become an essential part of the Liberian economy, but Lewis felt that such a program was basically an escape from the deeper issues of race and equality. When the school of immediate abolitionism arose, the Tappans soon transferred their allegiance (and financial support!) to this more radical approach.

When William Lloyd Garrison was imprisoned for libel, Arthur Tappan bailed him out. The resulting contact with Garrison and his thought drew Tappan toward immediate abolitionism and generated a small contribution toward the founding of the *Liberator*. Lewis was drawn into the movement by Theodore Weld. Finney had suggested that Tappan send his sons to the Oneida Institute in western New York. Oneida was operated by Finney's theological mentor, George Washington Gale, and the Tappan boys were converted there under the influence of Weld. When Lewis Tappan came up for commencement exercises, he met Weld, and the two men soon became close friends and coworkers in the antislavery struggle.

These growing convictions climaxed in the 1833 founding of the New York Anti-Slavery Society by the Tappans, Garrison, and a number of other revival and reform leaders. Though Arthur had been a major contributor to its construction, the trustees of Clinton Hall objected to his leasing the building for an abolitionist meeting, forcing a last-minute move to Finney's Chatham Street Chapel. While a mob mistakenly gathered outside Clinton Hall, the abolitionists in the church quickly adopted a constitution and elected Arthur Tappan president before dispersing into the night. A few abolitionists who had retired to an upstairs Sunday school room had to be rescued by the police when the mob discovered they had been misled and descended upon the church.

By the end of the year, sufficient interest had been generated to found a national society. Sixty delegates gathered in Philadelphia to promulgate a "Declaration of Sentiments" authored by Garrison that included the pledge to do "all that in us lies, consistently with this Declaration of our principles, to overthrow the most execrable system of slavery that has ever been witnessed upon earth . . . and to secure to the colored population of the United States, all the rights and privileges which belong to them as men, and as Americans—come what may to our persons, our interest, or our reputations." Arthur Tappan was also elected president of this new society, and the American Anti-Slavery Society had come into being.

Meanwhile the Tappans had been supporting Theodore Weld and a new seminary in Cincinnati that they hoped would become a citadel in the West of their revivalist and reform ideals. But when Lane Seminary trustees forbade the discussion of slavery, and Weld and his supporters withdrew rather than submit, Arthur Tappan shifted his support to the Lane Rebels and reneged on his commitment to the seminary. When Oberlin College emerged as a refuge for the radical students, Tappan convinced Finney to accept the professorship of theology, a chair that he offered to underwrite financially. Tappan also laid down the condition that Oberlin remain committed to "the broad ground of moral reform, in all its departments" and admit black students on an equal basis with whites.

Oberlin was very important to Tappan. He pledged his entire income (about one hundred thousand dollars a year—quite a sum in those days!) to the project, holding back only enough to provide modestly for his family. Unfortunately the business collapse of 1837 prevented Arthur from fulfilling his pledge. But by that time the school had been launched, and as Finney later put it, "Although Arthur Tappan failed to do for Oberlin all that he intended, yet his *promise* was the condition of the existence of Oberlin *as it has been*," the major center of antislavery activity in the West and a crucial force in the abolitionizing of the North.

Tappan money and organizational skill were also behind the abolitionist propaganda campaigns. Lewis Tappan created the plan of publishing four monthly journals (one to be issued each week) to be mailed free to influential persons throughout the country. This more than any other abolitionist activity united the South in opposition. Mobs broke into post offices to destroy shipments of the journals.

The Tappans had already come to expect such resistance. A mob had earlier ransacked Lewis's home, burning his furniture in the streets. (Mrs. Tappan found a bright spot in the event: the mob had destroyed some expensive-looking items that Lewis had always felt were too ostentatious for the frequent prayer meetings held in the home.) Tappan left his home unrepaired all summer as a "silent Anti-Slavery preacher to the crowds who will flock to see it." But this was nothing compared to the opposition to the postal campaign.

Southern officials insisted on the extradition of Arthur Tappan to face charges of fomenting a slave rebellion. One southern minister offered one hundred thousand dollars for the deliverance to New Orleans of Arthur Tappan and abolitionist editor La Roy Sunderland (later a founder of the abolitionist Wesleyan Methodist Connection; see chap. 7). Tappan responded to this offer with a rare burst of humor, "If that sum is placed in a New York bank, I may possibly think of giving myself up." The Tappans lived in fear of assassination or destruction of their property. They had to seek insurance out of the city in Boston at an "abolitionist premium." When the South began to boycott the Tappan's business enterprises and threatened the broadening of economic sanctions to those with whom they did business, the New York business community panicked and sent delegates to plead with the Tappans to give up their antislavery labors. To one party of this steady procession of visitors Arthur Tappan was heard to reply, "You demand that I shall cease my anti-slavery labors. . . . *I will be hung first*." Opposition seemed only to steel the Tappan brothers in their convictions, propelling them into ever more controversial involvements.

Lewis Tappan, for example, became a major figure in the Amistad Case. The *Amistad* (Spanish for "friendship") was a ship that had been built especially for the slave trade. While being transported from Cuba to Granaja, nearly fifty slaves had mutinied, killing the captain and the cook and imprisoning the Cuban crew. Under the leadership of Joseph Cinqué (apparently the source of the name adopted by "General Field Marshall Cinque" of the Patty Hearst kidnappers), the Africans tried to sail for Africa while the Cubans tried to alter the course toward a sympathetic state in the South. The ship ended up near Long Island where the United States Navy seized it.

This incident gripped the attention not only of the American public, but the whole Western world. American prejudices against Africans were strong (were they not murderers and perhaps even cannibals?), and major questions about the future of the slave trade would depend on how the United States government handled the case. Lewis Tappan immediately formed a committee for the defense of the blacks and took upon himself their physical and spiritual care. He carried the case all the way to the Supreme Court and then raised money to send the blacks back to their homes in Africa—along with a few missionaries from Oberlin.

The Amistad Case led directly into another philanthropy of Lewis Tappan. The Tappan brothers had become increasingly disenchanted with the benevolent societies. The American Bible Society had refused to make slaves and freedmen particular objects of Scripture distribution. The American Tract Society had not only refused to issue abolitionist tracts, but had edited out offending passages in British materials. The missionary societies did not hesitate to send out proslavery missionaries. After failing in his efforts to change such practices, Lewis Tappan finally moved toward founding a separate antislavery missionary society. The Amistad committee was merged into a few other organizations to form the American Missionary Association a "living protest" against the societies that refused to take a stand on slavery.

Lewis Tappan said of the AMA that "its single object is to send out a pure gospel free from any compromise." The AMA supported as many as two hundred missionaries (including a number sent to the South) and expended a million dollars in its first decade. Though not always able to break completely out of the paternalistic mold, this society was far in advance of its time. Tappan asked abolitionist Amos Phelps for advice in running the West Indian mission. Among the principles advocated in Phelps's report was "dealing with the people in all things as men and not as serviles." This included enabling them to find economic self-sufficiency and encouraging the missionaries to avoid expensive, comfortable quarters to "identify themselves with the people."

The American Missionary Association attempted to express the goals of equality to which the Tappans had long been committed (often in advance of other abolitionists who wished to rid the country of the sin of slavery, but had no interest in "social intercourse"). For the Tappans the abolitionist struggle was not just against slavery but explicitly against "prejudice" and the "hateful caste feeling that so extensively prevailed in the country." Lewis Tappan was especially concerned that children be raised sensitive to the issue of race so that as adults they would "be able to meet at the polls, sit on juries, attend political meetings, practice at the bar, unite in processions, and mingle with their fellow-men in the various walks of life, on equal terms, as the religion of Jesus, and the laws of the land require."

These sentiments were touchingly expressed by Lewis Tappan at age seventy-five during an Emancipation Jubilee in 1863. After reviewing with some nostalgia the antislavery struggle, Lewis commented that some claimed that blacks were superior to whites in intelligence and strength, but Tappan wasn't so sure and believed that "a white man was just as good as a black man, if he behaved himself." After the cheers and laughter subsided, Tappan closed with a verse of poetry:

> Judge not of virtue by the name,
> Or think to read it on the skin;
> Honor in white and black the same—
> the stamp of glory is within.

7 Orange Scott, Luther Lee, and the Wesleyan Methodists

In January 1844, the *Oberlin Evangelist* took delight in noticing the appearance of a new paper being received on exchange. The *True Wesleyan* spoke for a group that had seceded the previous year from the Methodist Episcopal Church under the leadership of such men as Orange Scott, Jotham Horton, and Luther Lee. Of these men the *Evangelist* commented that "their open and fearless advocacy of the claims of truth, justice and downtrodden humanity, endeared them to the hearts of all true philanthropists" and of the paper that "in it, the claims of the Lord's poor and oppressed ones have their proper place."

Within the somewhat interrelated contexts of Congregationalism and Presbyterianism, Oberlin had led the abolitionist struggle without spinning off to form a new denomination (though it played a part in the New School/Old School split). Within Methodism, however, the antislavery struggle produced a new antislavery denomination, the Wesleyan Methodist Connection of America, surely one of the few churches in Christian history to be founded squarely on a social issue. The Wesleyan Methodists emerged explicitly as a protest against Methodist compromise on the question of slavery.

Early Methodism had been characterized by vigorous opposition to slavery. As early as 1743 Wesley had written into his "General Rules" a prohibition against "The buying and selling the bodies and souls of men, women and children, with an intention to enslave them." His 1774 *Thoughts upon Slavery* condemned

every gentleman that has an estate in our American plantations; *yea*, ALL SLAVEHOLDERS OF WHATEVER RANK AND DE-

GREE; *seeing men-buyers are exactly on a level with man-stealers. You therefore are guilty, yea* PRINCIPALLY GUILTY, *of all these frauds, robberies, and murders.* You are the spring that puts all the rest into motion.

Wesley's last letter, written just a few days before his death, encouraged William Wilberforce in his fight against "that execrable villainy" in these words: "Go on, in the name of God, and in the power of his might, till even American slavery (the vilest that ever saw the sun) shall vanish away before it."

American Methodism attempted at first to maintain these convictions. The 1784 founding conference of the Methodist Episcopal Church had called for the expulsion of any member engaging in the slave trade, but with the growth of Methodism into the largest American denomination, this stance was gradually abandoned. When faced with the alternative of growth into a national church or maintaining discipline on the slavery issue, Methodism chose growth and prosperity. By the 1820s and 1830s the Methodists had largely accommodated to the institution of slavery, maintaining at most a nominal disapproval preserved in the *Discipline*.

But the growth of abolitionism in the 1830s again sensitized the consciences of some Methodists. Foremost among these was Orange Scott. Born into a penniless Vermont home in 1800, Scott had received only a few scattered months of education and was not converted until the age of twenty-one. But he gave himself immediately to the Methodist ministry and, despite handicaps in background and education, developed into a powerful leader and preacher. By 1830 he was elected presiding elder (a sort of "district superintendent"), and some were beginning to predict that he would one day be a bishop.

But this promising church career was interrupted by a "crisis of conscience." At the age of thirty-three, Orance Scott became an abolitionist. Though "ashamed to confess it" later, Scott lamented that until that time he had been "ignorant of some important principles or features of civil rights." As he expressed himself years afterward on his deathbed, "being wholly devoted to the one idea of saving souls, I omitted to examine, faithfully and critically as I should, the condition of the country in respect to great moral evils. My eyes, however, were at length opened."

Scott studied the *Liberator* of William Lloyd Garrison and other abolitionist writings for a year before declaring himself an abolitionist. He then spent one hundred dollars of his own money (no small amount in that time for a Methodist preacher!) to subscribe to the *Liberator* for three months in the name of one hundred ministers of the New England Conference. Before the subscriptions expired, a majority of the conference had been "radicalized." As a result the New England delegation to the General Conference of 1836 was abolitionist and included Orange Scott.

Here real confrontation began, and Scott was propelled into national leadership as the key figure in extended debates on slavery. Though one observer characterized his debating as "a noble and lofty effort; calm, dignified, generous, Christian," his opponents insisted that Scott was either a "reckless incendiary or *non compos mentis*." One opponent was heard to mutter somewhat euphemistically on the conference floor, "I wish *to God* he were in heaven." But in spite of Scott's efforts, the conference delegates resolved (by a vote of 120 to 14) to express themselves as "decidedly opposed to modern abolitionism, and wholly disclaim any right, wish or intention to interfere in the Civil and political relationship between master and slave, as it exists in the slave-holding States of the Union." The intent of this motion was made clear when the conference refused an amendment proposed by Scott and others that would add words taken directly from the *Discipline* to the effect that "we are as much as ever convinced of the great evil of slavery."

This resolution became the excuse for the suppression of antislavery discussion within the Methodist Episcopal Church. That year Scott's bishop said that he would reappoint Scott to the presiding eldership only if he would cease lecturing and writing on the subject of slavery. Scott refused and was demoted. Elsewhere bishops and church leaders refused to allow antislavery resolutions to come to the floor of annual conferences, assigned abolitionist ministers either to "hard scrabble"

circuits or to churches where the antiabolitionist feeling was so
strong that they would be crushed, brought ministers to trial for
attending abolitionist meetings or even reading abolitionist literature, and so on.

Feelings were intense during this period. Those opposing
the abolitionists viewed them with real fear. One attack was
entitled *Abolition a Sedition* and protested the argument that
"slavery is wrong by a higher and more imperative law than that
of the country," insisting that such a position led to an unconsti-
tutional intrusion of religion into the civil realm. Abolitionism,
moreover, distorted the true nature of Christianity, for "it is to
the *conservative* power of Christianity that we owe our greatest
blessings." The author feared, too, that the abolitionist movement possessed the seeds of anarchy, because it advocated the
leveling of "all distinctions in society, of rank, color, caste, and
sex."

The tensions mounted. The abolitionists insisted that slavery
was "sin" and that the churches were the "bulwark of slavery."
Their opponents feared anarchy and saw the abolitionists as
"subversives" destroying all semblance of "law and order." The
pressures on the abolitionists became unbearable, and Scott
himself left the ministry for two years to serve as one of the
Seventy agents sent out by the American Anti-Slavery Society to
spread the gospel of abolitionism. But Scott insisted that though
"I closed up and left the 'regular work' of a stationed preacher
. . . I still profess to be engaged in the 'regular and appropriate
work' of a *gospel minister.*"

Scott returned to his church in 1839, but by this time sentiment was growing for the establishment of a new Methodist
body that was "truly Wesleyan" and unflinchingly devoted to
reform principles. At first these ministers tried to avoid the
charge of schism, arguing that it was more to the point to insist
that "anti-abolitionist measures tend to schism." But after a
long struggle Scott finally decided that there was no alternative
but to "stand forth for a new anti-slavery, anti-intemperance,
anti-everything-wrong church organization," and the Wesleyan
Methodist Connection was formed in the early 1840s.

It is difficult now to recreate the ethos and style of this new denomination. Though focused on the issue of slavery, they became "universal reformers." Their spirit can be seen in the title of an early hymnal *Miriam's Timbrel: Sacred Songs Suited to Revival Occasions; and also for Anti-Slavery, Peace, Temperance and Reform Meetings.* This hymnal consists of songs appropriate for each type of rally, as well as a general section of "Songs for the Reformer." Among the latter the following is typical:

> We will speak out. We will be heard,
>   Though all earth's systems crack.
> We will not bate a single word
>   Nor take a letter back.
>
> We speak the Truth, and what care we
>   For hissing and for scorn
> While some faint gleamings we can see
>   of freedom's coming morn.
>
> Let liars fear; let cowards shrink;
>   Let traitors turn away.
> Whatever we have dared to think
>   that dare we also say.

Wesleyans tested the spirituality of a church by its commitment to reform but refused to substitute reform for piety. Orange Scott warned the young church in 1845 that "deep Experience in the things of God is essential to the peace and usefulness of all Christians; but especially is it essential to any class of Christian Reformers." Wesleyans often spoke of the conjunction of "piety and radicalism," claiming to excell in both areas. The host pastor of the founding convention of the church had tried to assure the early Wesleyans that they would be welcome by affirming that "we believe there is sufficient piety and radicalism to entertain all who will attend."

Another characteristic of the Wesleyans was specificity in their attacks on social evil. Scott insisted that "in opposing sin, the power of the Gospel must be brought to bear upon *particular evils. Generalizing* will not answer. We must *particularize.*" And Scott believed in starting at home by attacking "*popular sins* and *sins of the Church.*"

The Wesleyans did not center their attack on the South. Scott insisted that "all northern Christians, who neglect to lift up the warning voice and *refuse to take sides* with God's suffering poor, *are scarcely less guilty.*" This involved a sense of "corporate guilt" that is made explicit in a statement of George Pegler stating why he left the Methodist Protestants to join the Wesleyans. Though lengthy, its contemporary relevance and contradiction of the stereotypes of pietistic individualism justify more extensive quotation:

We believe that the churches of the North are responsible for the continuance of slavery . . .

First, the churches at the North, as well as at the South, hold the slave-holder in Christian fellowship, thus endorsing his Christian character and esteeming him as a brother beloved, and thus justifying his daily acts of man stealing.

Second, by members of the northern churches voting at elections for the man-thief, and his apologist, thus giving evidence that they approve of the wicked laws they enact, whereby they oppress the poor. This is done every year. And the church approves of these acts, and is thus striking hands with the oppressor instead of being a reprover of those who commit the deeds of darkness.

Third, the members of the northern churches sustain those parties that make those civil laws which crush the poor colored man in their midst; and among those who are victims of this cruel class legislation are many who are members of their own church.

Fourth, in most of the churches at the North the "negro pew" is erected, thus showing that they despise the poor, and have "become respectors of persons."

Fifth, but few of the churches at the North will allow their doors to be open to plead the cause of the poor and oppressed. They are willing to hear harangues in praise of Henry Clay, or Martin Van Buren, or any slave-holder or his apologist, but the man who will dare to open his mouth for the dumb or attempt to exhibit the wickedness and wrongs of slavery will have the door shut in his face; or if he be allowed to speak, his views will be distorted and himself held up to ridicule; or maybe he will be represented as a Traitor to his country, and enemy to republicanism, and often be in personal danger from the fury of a pro-slavery mob, headed by officers and prominent members of a Christian church.

But this emphasis on the role of the Northern churches must not be taken to mean that the Wesleyans were afraid to tackle slavery directly. In 1847 Adam Crooks answered a call to North Carolina. He wrote in his diary, "I turned my face to go to the far south, to pronounce that Gospel which proclaims liberty to the captives, and the opening of the prisons to them that are bound." Such "missionaries" were mobbed, dragged into court, and imprisoned. At least one Wesleyan minister in the South was lynched. But these preachers set about founding churches with such names as Freedom Hill and Lovejoy Memorial Chapel. (Lovejoy was an abolitionist editor killed by a mob wishing to destroy his paper.) Crooks wrote back from the South that "opposition to my course is great. My image was tarred and feathered in this town . . . some of my friends are beginning to tremble for my personal safety; but my trust is in the Friend of the poor, the Deliverer of the oppressed." Crooks eventually had to leave the state to escape imprisonment on the charge of

with force and arms, knowingly, wickedly, and unlawfully, with intention to excite insurrection, conspiracy, and resistance in the slaves and free negroes and persons of color within the state, bringing into the state with the intention to circulate, a printed pamphlet named and styled the "Ten Commandments."

Orange Scott unfortunately met an early death in 1847. There circulates among some Wesleyans today the rumor that on his deathbed Scott renounced his "worldly" reform activities, but his memoirs reveal otherwise. He regretted that his responsibilities in the "book business" had become so consuming. He wished that he had given up that work and carried out his original plans. He regretted he had not given himself more fully to the oppressed and fought for a reordering of society on their behalf. In his own words,

I should have gone into the work of impressing on the wealthy classes, their duty to the millions enduring poverty and toil. I feel deeply for that class, and would do my share in carrying forward a practical plan of reform, according to my means. The condition of the masses is wretched indeed, and a great change should be effected in the state of society. It might be done if a few strong men would take hold of it in the pulpit and elsewhere.

Scott's death forced others into leadership of the new denomination. Among these was Luther Lee, who had been born November 30, 1800, into an impoverished upstate New York home. At nineteen Lee reaffirmed the faith of his childhood and, though nearly illiterate, moved toward the Methodist ministry. After several years in frontier circuits and efforts to overcome his lack of education, he rose to leadership, largely because of his powers as a revivalist and his ability in debate. (Lee gained quite a reputation for debating Universalist ministers on the question of universal salvation.)

In 1837 Lee became an abolitionist and immediately threw himself into the antislavery struggle. "Logical Lee," as he came to be called, was especially in demand to defend ministers in church trials for such offenses as "agitating the slavery question" or "patronizing abolitionist publications." After a period of service as an agent of the Massachusetts Abolition Society and helping to organize the antislavery Liberty party in 1840, Lee joined Orange Scott and others in founding Wesleyan Methodism.

Lee presided over three of the first six general conferences of the new denomination, edited the *True Wesleyan*, and defended church positions in various writings. He also wrote a number of shorter theological works (attacking Unitarianism and defending the immortality of the soul against "conditionalism" that affirmed that only Christians received immortality) as well as a systematic theology that went through a dozen editions. Lee later served the Wesleyans as professor of theology at Adrian College before returning to the Methodist Episcopal Church after the Civil War.

Lee left behind several volumes of sermons (*The Evangelical Pulpit, 1854–1864*) and a number published in pamphlet form. These materials provide insight into Wesleyan preaching in an era when the social gospel was still a part of Evangelicalism.

Lee's understanding of the relationship of preaching to public issues is seen in a late (ca. 1864) sermon on "The radicalism of the Gospel." There he argued the basic thesis that "THE GOS-PEL IS SO RADICALLY REFORMATORY, THAT TO PREACH IT FULLY AND CLEARLY, IS TO ATTACK AND CONDEMN ALL WRONG, AND TO ASSERT AND DEFEND ALL RIGHTEOUSNESS."

Lee defended this position by "denying all neutrality or middle ground" and quoted the words of Jesus: "He that is not with me is against me" (Matt. 12:30). He maintained that the "Gospel asserts its radical reform position, by demanding absolute obedience and submission." Lee opposed all decisions based on "expedience," insisting that "right must be responded to, regardless of worldly considerations." He argued that "ministers, Christians, and churches, lose their moral power when they fail to exemplify the whole gospel." Therefore, "reformers should be reformed," just as "to promote a revival of religion, we must have the elements of a revival in our own breasts."

Lee was certain that "the gospel will never reform mankind, only so far as it is applied specifically to the evils to be removed." This would immediately involve entering the political arena. Lee insisted that "a large portion of the evils are connected with civil government, and the gospel will never remove them, until it is so preached as to have something to do with politics." (On the other hand, Lee insisted in his autobiography that "I never had any politics which were not a part of my religion, and I urged men to vote the Liberty ticket as a religious duty.")

With this background, one can understand the sermons Lee preached in response to some of the great events of his day. Lee himself was radicalized by the death of Rev. Elijah P. Lovejoy, an abolitionist editor shot by a mob trying to silence him by destroying his press for the fourth time. Until this time Lee had assumed that since abolitionists were "attacked by the religious press . . . they must be a set of desperate fanatics." But upon the death of Lovejoy, Lee was "stirred, and judged it wrong to remain silent any longer." As Lee put it later, "I preached a sermon on the death of Mr. Lovejoy, in which I condemned all

mob violence, vindicated the principles for the utterance of
which Mr. Lovejoy had been killed, and condemned slavery as
an unmitigated wrong."

Among other questions Lee asked, "Suppose the promulga-
tion of Abolition principles does really endanger the slave-hold-
ers of the south, where does the fault rest? On the Abolitionist,
or on the slave-holding system?" A racist society blamed the
abolitionist for tearing it apart. The abolitionists insisted on
throwing the blame back onto society and its sins.

A decade later Lee preached another sermon that revealed
how much the issues had changed. This sermon was evoked by
the death of Rev. Charles Turner Torrey in a Baltimore prison
while serving a sentence for invading the South to help slaves
escape. Those like Lee who took an active part in the underground railroad had to face the fact, as had Oberlin, that such
activities were illegal under the federal fugitive slave laws. And
Lee followed the course that Oberlin had taken by developing a
doctrine of civil disobedience that appealed to the "higher law."

Lee expressed this position in his sermon entitled "The Su-
premacy of the Divine Law." After urging the right of the slaves
to freedom on the basis of the Scriptures and "unalienable
rights" (that is, on the basis of the Declaration of Independ-
ence), Lee praised Torrey for "placing the law of God and the
claims of his Maker above all human law, and the praise or the
wrath of men."

Lee also defended Torrey against his more "friendly" de-
tractors. Lee was convinced that

no man can at this day and in this country, rise up and contend for
all that is right in politics and religion, and carry out by consistent
action the principles for which he contends without being accused
of rashness by his opposers, and suspected of indiscretion by his
pretended friends.

Again like Oberlin, Lee found that this position pushed him
to support John Brown's raid on Harper's Ferry. Brown's action
was in effect a form of guerilla warfare—he had hoped that the
slaves would rise up and join him in throwing off the yoke of
oppression.

Lee responded to Brown's execution by preaching a sermon entitled "Dying to the Glory of God." Here again, he appealed both to biblical example and to the precedent of the American Revolution to argue that in some cases "it is right to oppose oppression, and defend human liberty . . . by force and arms." This position amounted to a rationale for a "just revolution" in the face of oppression.

This sermon apparently came to the attention of the family of John Brown, for the following July 4 Lee was invited to deliver another oration from the rock overlooking Brown's grave in North Elba, New York. Lee himself called it "the oration of my life, the most radical and, probably, the most able I ever delivered." Unfortunately this speech did not survive. Lee loaned the manuscript to a reporter and never saw it again.

But another sermon, more than any other, assured Lee of a place in history. Luther Lee preached the ordination sermon for Antoinette Brown, apparently the first woman in history to be fully ordained to the Christian ministry. Rev. Brown was, as has been mentioned, a graduate of Oberlin, where she had also studied theology. Lee had been a major defender of the women delegates who had tried to be seated at various temperance conventions. Antoinette Brown had been among these delegates and apparently asked Lee to preach because of those contacts.

So on September 15, 1853, Luther Lee preached a sermon entitled "Woman's Right to Preach the Gospel." He argued exegetically that there was no valid objection to the ordination of women on biblical grounds. This involved a number of steps (making explicit the major roles of women in the New Testament and the early church, arguing that in the relevant Pauline passages, "the apostle's injunction was not given as a general rule, but as a remedy for a specific difficulty," etc.). But the heart of his argument was based on his text (Gal. 3:28—a verse that had been crucial for Lee's antislavery sentiments as well): "There is neither Jew nor Greek, there is neither bond nor free, there is neither male nor female; for ye are all one in Christ Jesus."

It is difficult to know how to evaluate the Wesleyans. How can we put the discussion into contemporary terms? A racist and slaveholding society viewed the abolitionists as insurrectionists. Perhaps that was not inappropriate. Donald G. Mathews, a recent student of Scott, suggests that to

call him a reformer would be to misunderstand his importance; rather, he was a revolutionary. . . . He opposed a whole system. He demanded not the reform of slavery, but its abolition, and in doing so, implied the destruction of Southern and even American society as he and his contemporaries knew it. The implication of the abolitionist preaching was a new kind of society much different from the old—an implication only gradually being realized in the 20th century.[1]

Orange Scott, Luther Lee, and the Wesleyan Methodists have been vindicated in recent years. What appeared as revolution and insurrection to their contemporaries now appears to us to have been responsible social witness. With clear foresight Luther Lee predicted this in his sermon preached on the death of Orange Scott in 1847:

If it be insisted that he was ultra and rash, it was because he lived in advance of his age. He advocated no sentiments, and resorted to no measures, which are not destined, very soon, to become the moderate sober views of the world.

1. Donald G. Matthews, "Orange Scott: The Methodist Evangelist As Revolutionary," in *The Anti-Slavery Vanguard: New Essays on the Abolitionists*, ed. Martin Duberman (Princeton: Princeton University Press, 1965), p. 100.

8   The Evangelical Roots
of Feminism

The same twists of history that have obscured the Evangelical
sources of abolitionism have also hidden the early Evangelical
commitment to feminist principles. By and large, today's
Evangelicals have been dead set against the recent movement of
women's liberation. The ordination of women has been opposed
by the dominant leaders of contemporary Evangelicalism. The
Christian bookstores today are filled with innumerable books
affirming traditional roles for women, emphasizing the subordination of women to men, and calling Evangelical women to a
"total" and "fascinating" womanhood that completely sub-
merges their own personalities and aspirations.

Here again, evangelist Billy Graham typifies the current
Evangelical attitude. Writing for the *Ladies' Home Journal* he
affirmed that

the biological assignment was basic and simple: Eve was to be the
child-bearer, and Adam was to be the breadwinner. . . . Wife,
mother, homemaker—this is the appointed destiny of real womanhood.[1]

Similar sentiments are echoed by his wife Ruth Graham, who
responded in the pages of *Christianity Today* to the ordination of
women in these words:

I personally am "agin it." For one thing, I do not feel that we have
much of a shortage of men. For another thing, I believe that it
basically goes against the principles of Scripture. . . . I think if you
study you will find that the finest cooks in the world are men (probably called chefs); the finest couturiers, by and large are men; the

1. Billy Graham, "Jesus and the Liberated Woman," *Ladies' Home
Journal*, December 1970, p. 42.

greatest politicians are men; most of our greatest writers are men; most of our greatest athletes are men. You name it, men are superior in all but two areas: women make the best wives and women make the best mothers.[2]

The irony of such statements is that modern revivalism gave birth to the women's rights movement. A recent anthology of *The Feminist Papers* collected by Alice Rossi begins to set the record straight by tracing the roots of American feminism to the revivalism of Charles G. Finney and the reform movements it spawned.[3] This theme is repeated by Beverly Wildung Harrison of Union Theological Seminary in New York, who asserts:

The fact is that the social origins of the woman's rights movement in America will not be fully or adequately understood, nor the early feminists rightly appreciated, until the connection is duly acknowledged between the woman movement and left-wing Reformation evangelicalism in America. It is to Rossi's credit that she is one of the first contemporary feminists to identify the connection between the Second Great Awakening, in which Charles Finney himself was moved to support women's right to pray and testify, and the woman's rights movement.[4]

Actually, it is Evangelicalism that next to Quakerism has given the greatest role to women in the life of the church. This practice crested in nineteenth-century American revivalism but was foreshadowed in the Evangelical Revival of the preceding century. The reasons for this are complex, and some have already been suggested. There is an implicit leveling force in vital Evangelical religion. Some have even argued that the Evangelical Revival transmitted to English society the radical egalitarian ideas that fomented modern revolutions in other contexts. This leveling impact contributed to the rise of the laity in church life, and in this process, women found new roles earlier denied them

2. Ruth Graham, comment in "Others Say . . ." column, *Christianity Today*, 6 June 1975, p. 32.

3. Alice Rossi, *The Feminist Papers* (New York: Columbia University Press, 1974; paperback, Bantam Books, 1974), part 2.

4. Beverly Wildung Harrison, "The Early Feminists and the Clergy: A Case Study in the Dynamics of Secularization," *Review and Expositor*, Winter 1975, p. 46.

just as laymen were allowed to preach and take other forms of leadership.

The Evangelical turn to Christian experience also helped open new vistas for women. Such an emphasis undercut the traditional sources of religious authority—trained clergy, ecclesiastical hierarchies, sacramental systems, and so on. When a high premium was placed on sensitivity to religious growth and personal interaction in small groups, it was discovered that women, though denied formal theological training, had a knack for leadership in such contexts. In fact, women by virtue of their socialization (if not inherent qualities) were more attuned to the emotional and personal factors involved in growth through the religious "stages in life's way."

There was also a certain innovative and experimental thrust to Evangelicalism that found expression in such new and strange practices as "field preaching" in the case of George Whitefield, or in setting hymns to popular and contemporary tunes in the case of the Wesleys. These new practices were justified in part pragmatically by whether they worked or not. Wesley himself, a rigidly conventional Oxford Don by nature, despised field preaching until he saw how many were converted by its use. After passing through the trauma of breaking into such new practices, Evangelicals were able to look back and see that their resistance had been cultural conditioning rather than some absolute understanding derived from the core of biblical faith.

In this way Evangelicals began to experiment with new roles for women in the church. Wesley himself gave approval to a few women preachers by the end of his life. And in America the Great Awakenings so reproduced the same phenomena that by the end of the eighteenth century women preachers had begun to appear in such groups as the Free-Will Baptists. Evangelicals did not continue in these practices without testing them against scriptural exegesis, but they found that by approaching the Scriptures with unbiased eyes it became clear that women had played a more significant role in the New Testament church than had previously been assumed, and that a biblical case could be made for giving them more responsibilities in the contemporary church. By the beginning of the nineteenth century new conclusions were being expressed in standard reference works. Adam Clarke's highly influential commentary on the Bible, for example, affirmed of women that "under the blessed spirit of Christianity, they have equal *rights*, equal *privileges*, and equal *blessings*, and let me add, they are equally *useful*."

But it was in the American revivalism of Charles G. Finney that such tendencies began to have wide cultural impact and were transformed into the practice of full ordination for women and a form of Christian and biblical feminism. As already indicated, the most controversial of Finney's "new measures" in his revivals was his encouragement of women to speak and pray in public and mixed meetings. Theodore Weld apparently helped push Finney in this direction. The week of his conversion in 1825 Weld had encouraged the women to speak, and one night "seven females, a number of them the most influential Christians in the city, confessed their sin in being restrained by their sex and prayed publickly in succession." Finney's own commitment to the practice was revealed in the 1827 New Lebanon Conference called to reconcile Finney with the more conservative revivalists from New England. Though allowing women to speak in public assemblies was the most volatile topic of dissension, Finney refused to back down.

We have already seen how Oberlin College became the first coeducational college in the world and one of the few places encouraging women to get a college education. Asa Mahan, Oberlin's first president, was so proud of this record that he suggested for a tombstone epitaph the one fact that he was "the first man, in the history of the race who conducted women, in connection with members of the opposite sex, through a full course of liberal education, and conferred upon her the high degrees which had hitherto been the exclusive preogatives of men." Antoinette Brown, the first woman to be ordained, remembered Mahan toward the end of her life as "unusually liberal even for the more liberal men of his day."

Oberlin graduated a number of the leaders of feminism. These women later complained that Oberlin had still been a little stuffy and unwilling to go as far as they wished, but it was in the revivalist context that they first found the door to new vistas slightly ajar. Lucy Stone, Oberlin class of 1847, refused to take her husband's name in marriage and was known as "Mrs. Stone." Her name became an epithet used in derision of the "strange creatures" who broke this social convention. At their wedding, she and her husband Henry Blackwell together signed a protest declaring that their marriage implied "no sanction of, nor promise of voluntary obedience to such of the present laws of marriage, as refuse to recognize the wife as an independent, rational being, while they confer upon the husband an injurious and unnatural superiority, investing him with legal powers which no man should possess." Later in 1870 the same couple founded the *Woman's Journal*, the principal suffragist paper.

But the abolitionist controversy enabled a genuine feminism to emerge. Just as the civil rights movement of the 1960s contributed to the modern reemergence of feminism, in the 1830s abolitionism spawned the woman's rights movement. There would seem to be several reasons for this connection. The basic egalitarianism of evangelicalism that supported abolitionism was also extended to women. Those who had mustered the courage to attack one social institution found it easier to attack another. Women who mastered the antislavery argument found unexpected parallels to their own situation. But probably most important for the Evangelicals were the parallel problems in the interpretation of Scripture.

The Grimké sisters, Angelina and Sarah, made the initial breakthroughs. Their religious history is complex and still not entirely sorted out. Though usually identified as Quakers, they were originally converted from Southern aristocratic Episcopalianism under the influence of Presbyterian revivalism. They apparently turned to Quakerism because that sect most fully expressed their newfound antislavery sentiments. As we have seen, Angelina later became the wife of Theodore Weld. It was in their work with Weld and the Seventy that the Grimké sisters faced severe opposition from the traditional clergy who argued against women speaking in public to quash their antislavery agitation. Sarah and Angelina were then forced to defend their work.

Sarah Grimké soon developed her feminist principles in *Letters on the Equality of the Sexes*, originally published in 1837. This work explicitly described parallels between the state of the slave and the condition of women. Sarah Grimké signed her letters "Thine in the bonds of womanhood" and suggested that "the cupidity of man soon led him to regard women as property," pointing out that in some parts of the world women were sold into marriage just as slaves. One letter sketched the laws of the age which left "women very little more liberty, or power, in some respects, than the slave." She also claimed that "in all ages and countries, woman has more or less been made a *means* to promote the welfare of man, without regard to her own happiness, and the glory of God, as the end of her creation."

But the argument still turned for Evangelicals on biblical interpretation. It was abolitionists who discovered "feminist exegesis." The abolitionists faced conservatives who built a "Bible defense of slavery" on biblical instances of slavery and biblical admonitions to obedience on the part of slaves. Those who mastered Theodore Weld's "Bible argument against slavery" and learned to defend the egalitarian and liberationist "spirit" of the Bible against status quo literal interpretations, found that the same arguments could be used in support of the women's movement. Even Galatians 3:28 seemed to conjoin the issues by declaring that "There is neither Jew nor Greek there is neither bond nor free, there is neither male nor female; for ye are all one in Christ Jesus."

The full hermeneutical and theological significance of these moves was not spelled out until later in the century, but the Grimké sisters began immediately to push for more appropriate translations of the Scriptures, pointing out that men had often unconsciously imported sexist distortions into their work. Of the New Testament Sarah insisted, "I am willing to abide by its decision, and must enter my protest against the false translations of some passages by the MEN who did that work. . . .

When we are admitted to the honor of studying Greek and Hebrew, we shall produce some versions of the Bible, a little different from those we have now." Illustrative of the kind of retranslation she called for is her comment on the early chapters of Genesis. "The literal translation of the word 'help-meet' is a helper like unto himself; and is so rendered in the Septuagint and manifestly signifies a companion."

Out of these currents flowed a stream of feminism that engulfed much of Evangelicalism by the end of the century. In the first generation or so, feminism was found largely in those groups that had been most firmly committed to abolitionism, but by the second generation such convictions had gained a momentum of their own that went beyond the circles that remembered the antislavery struggle.

The Wesleyan Methodists, for example, had striking connections with the woman's rights movement. The Seneca Falls meeting of 1848 that launched the movement and first called for the franchise for women was held in a Wesleyan Methodist church—apparently because only the abolitionist denomination was at all receptive to such radical ideas. (Even here there was some equivocation. When the women arrived for the meeting, they found the building locked and had to climb in through a window!) We have already mentioned that Luther Lee of the Wesleyans preached the ordination sermon for Antoinette Brown, the first woman to be fully ordained—even though she was a Congregationalist. Lee appears regularly in the literature of the movement for his efforts to defend women who attempted to attend temperance conventions as full voting delegates.

The convictions that Lee expressed in the ordination sermon entitled "Woman's Right to Preach the Gospel" can only be called feminist. Interpreting Galatians 3:28, he insisted that "I cannot see how the text can be explained so as to exclude females from any right, office, work, privilege, or immunity which males enjoy, hold or perform. If the text means anything, it means that males and females are equal in rights, privileges and responsibilities upon the Christian Platform." In the next decade (the 1860s) some Wesleyan Methodists began to ordain women, nearly a century in advance of the Methodist

Episcopal Church. The practice was debated for the rest of the century before becoming relatively common in the early years of the twentieth century.

Though he did not speak much on the issue, Presbyterian/ Congregationalist Jonathan Blanchard of Wheaton College seems to have shared some of these feminist convictions. In his Cincinnati debate with N. L. Rice, he proclaimed that "the first alteration which Christianity made in the polity of Judaism was to abrogate this oppressive distinction of sexes" in which "women had almost no rights; they were menials to their husbands and parents."

Blanchard and Lee both seem to have preserved the teaching that "the husband is the head of the wife," but others went beyond this to advocate an egalitarian marriage relationship. Among these was B. T. Roberts, founder of the Free Methodist Church, another split from the Methodist Episcopal Church over, at least in part, the question of slavery. Though his denomination did not capitulate to the full ordination of women until 1974 (a fact he profoundly regretted), in 1891 Roberts authored one of the most radical of the Evangelical defenses of feminism.

In marriage Roberts urged the model of the business partnership: "The greatest domestic happiness always exists where husband and wife live together on terms of equality. Two men, having individual interests, united only by business ties, daily associate as partners for years, without either of them being in subjection to the other. They consider each other as equals. Then, cannot a man and woman, united in conjugal love, the strongest tie that can unite two human beings having *the same* interests, live together in the same manner?" Roberts's book also explicitly dealt with the hermeneutical issues involved in a "biblical feminism" and argued the parallel with the problem of slavery.

Another Free Methodist bishop, W. A. Sellew, pursued the same issues in *Why Not?* (1894). He claimed that "women the world over have been patiently waiting . . . for the glorious gospel of love, as taught by Jesus Christ and its attendant civilization, to restore to her those rights which have been taken from her by force." He also advocated laws "permitting her to earn and own property and manage her personal business affairs untramelled by a class of men who think they possess superior knowledge on how a woman's money should be spent."

Baptist A. J. Gordon provides an interesting variation on these themes. Gordon was the major figure behind what has developed into Gordon College and Gordon-Conwell Theological Seminary, the major Evangelical educational institutions in New England. His son and biographer indicates that Gordon had "been bred in the strictest sect of the abolitionists" and with regard to women "advocated their complete enfranchisement and their entrance into every political and social privilege enjoyed by men."

When conservatives objected to women speaking at missionary conventions, Gordon responded in an essay on "The Ministry of Women" in the *Missionary Review of the World* (1894). There he argued that "in every great spiritual awakening in the history of Protestantism the impulse for Christian women to pray and witness for Christ in the public assembly has been found irrepressible." Gordon's essay is largely exegetical in character, but he argued more from Acts 2 than from the usual text of Galatians 3:28. Particular weight was given to a quotation from the Old Testament Book of Joel to the effect that "in the last days, saith God, I will pour forth of my Spirit upon all flesh; and your sons *and your daughters* shall prophecy."

Recent study has uncovered a major role of women in the early years of the Evangelical Free church, a Scandinavian immigrant denomination formed in the late nineteenth century, known today primarily through its seminary, Trinity Evangelical Divinity School, one of the largest and most prominent of the Evangelical seminaries. In a widely distributed pamphlet entitled "The Prophesying Daughters," Fredrick Franson, an early leader of the movement and founder of the Evangelical Alliance Mission (TEAM), defended the right of women to preach. In early years of the church a number of women served, not only as traveling evangelists, but also as stationed pastors. Full ordination of women was clearly intended in early constitutions, and the 1925 rules for ordination utilized such nonsexist

phraseology as "a candidate for ordination shall request a reference from the church of which he or she is a member relative to
the candidate's character, abilities, training and anything that
pertains to his or her call." The first women to avail themselves
of this opportunity included Christina Carlson, Ellen Modin,
Amanda Nelson, Carrie Norgaard, Hilma Severin, and Amanda
Gustafson.

But it was the Salvation Army that made the most progress in
putting such convictions into practice. This was due to the influence of Catherine Mumford Booth, cofounder of the army,
though many historians hardly mention her. Catherine had at
one point nearly refused to marry William Booth when he re-
marked in a letter that "woman has a fibre more in the heart
and a cell less in the brain." She insisted that lack of training
and opportunity were solely responsible for woman's secondary
place in society, and finally agreed to marriage only after William had accepted feminist convictions.

Catherine entered the fray over "women preachers" in the
1850s, writing letters to church papers and authoring a thirty-
two-page pamphlet entitled "Female Ministry" that had several
editions. She too argued from Pentecost that "the Spirit was
given to the female as to the male disciple . . . what a remarkable device of the devil that he has succeeded in hiding this . . .
but the time of her deliverance draweth nigh," and lamented
that "it is impossible to estimate the extent of the church's loss,
where prejudice and custom are allowed to render the outpour-
ing of God's spirit upon His handmaidens null and void."

When William became sick, Catherine substituted for him in
the pulpit and soon developed an important preaching ministry
of her own. Most reports suggest that she was better in the
pulpit than her husband. Often they would split up to "double
their power for good" and hold simultaneous preaching missions. In Portsmouth crowds averaging one thousand people
came nightly for seventeen weeks to hear her preach, and she
often spoke to much larger meetings.

When she had children, Catherine was careful to encourage
enlightened attitudes concerning women's roles. "I have tried to
grind it into my boys that their sisters were just as intelligent

and capable as themselves. Jesus Christ's principles were to put woman on the same platform as men, although I am sorry to say His apostles did not always act upon it." When her daughters were grown and married, they kept the Booth family name by hyphenating it to form Booth-Tucker, Booth-Clibborn, and so on. With such convictions motivating the Salvation Army, it is little wonder that egalitarian principles were built into the structure of the army from the beginning and that in 1934 Evangeline Booth was elected to the highest office of the army, that of general.

Nineteenth-century Evangelical literature contains intimations of other radical ideas now coming into their own. A. B. Simpson, founder of the Christian and Missionary Alliance, rejected the idea that Christ's incarnation was as a male. In *Echoes of the New Creation* he argued that "His humanity was unique and different from all other humanity. He is not a man, but He is *the* Man. He is not a male. He is just as much a woman as He is a man."

Others suggested the use of female imagery to describe God. Among these was Hannah Whitall Smith, author of the widely read religious classic *The Christian's Secret of a Happy Life*. "H.W.S." was a popular Bible teacher and with her husband, Robert, was a major force behind British Keswick Conventions calling Christians to a deeper spiritual life. She was also a frequent speaker at suffrage conventions and an ardent advocate of women's education. One of her Bible studies in *The Open Secret* is entitled "God As Our Mother." In this study she analyzed the "many . . . ways in which God is like a mother" in order to "open our eyes to see some truths concerning Him, which have been hitherto hidden from our gaze."

One cannot discuss Evangelical feminism without taking note of Frances Willard, a Methodist crusader who used the Women's Christian Temperance Union to provide a political outlet for women and to fight for the franchise. It was perhaps Frances Willard rather than more radical feminists who made suffrage palatable to the masses by tying the issue into "temperance" and "home protection." But Frances Willard also argued for the ordination of women in *Woman in the Pulpit* (1888) and called for sexually inclusive language in worship, complaining that "preachers almost never refer to the women of their audiences, but tell about 'men' and what 'a man' was and is and is to be."

Similar convictions and practices appear in other Evangelical traditions. Lee Anna Starr, Methodist Protestant pastor at Adrian College, authored *The Bible Status of Woman* (1926), a painstaking analysis of the relevant biblical texts. This book was published by Revell, the Evangelical publisher associated with the Moody revivals. Methodist medical doctor and reformer Katherine Bushnell spent the latter years of her life working in the original languages to produce books and pamphlets vindicating the Scriptures and defending feminism. Pentecostal traditions boast the ministries of Mary Woodworth-Etter, whom some now consider a founder of Pentecostalism, and Aimee Semple McPherson, founder of the International Church of the Foursquare Gospel.

But it was, however, the denominations produced by the mid-nineteenth-century "holiness revival" that most consistently raised feminism to a central principle of church life. This movement largely emerged from the work of Methodist lay evangelist Phoebe Palmer. This neglected figure played a major role in the Revival of 1857–58 and its extension to the old world by four years of evangelism in the British Isles. But in the midst of these revival efforts she published a 421-page defense of the right of women to preach entitled *The Promise of the Father*. This work argued from the account of Pentecost and became the fountainhead of innumerable such arguments developed through the remainder of the nineteenth century and into the twentieth.

Nor was Phoebe Palmer the only woman evangelist in the formative years of the movement. Another neglected figure is the black ex-slave Mrs. Amanda Berry Smith, who preached around the world. Methodist Episcopal bishop J. M. Thoburn said of her work in India that "during the seventeen years that I have lived in Calcutta, I have known many famous strangers to visit the city, but I have never known anyone who could draw and hold so large an audience as Mrs. Smith." And of her personal impact on himself he commented, "I have learned more that has been of actual value to me as a preacher of Christian Truth from Amanda Smith than from any other person I have ever met."

The major organ of this movement, the *Guide to Holiness*, frequently considered the role of women in the church. Among the convictions upheld in its pages were: "Pentecost laid the axe at the root of social injustice. The text of Peter's sermon that marvelous day was the keynote of woman's enfranchisement." Objecting to the fact that woman "contents herself with shining, like the moon, with borrowed splendor, as the mother, sister, or wife of the great so-and-so. . . . She has left her talent in its napkin while she has been obeying the world's dictum by helping to make the most of his." "When the Pentecostal light shines most brightly, women do the bulk of the common-school teaching. They are also principals, professors, college presidents, and are admitted to all the learned professions. . . . When the light shines clearly, they have equal rights with men by whose side they labor for God's glory."

With such sentiments in the early years of the holiness movement, it is not surprising that the "holiness" denominations that formed later at the turn of the century institutionalized feminist principles. The Church of God (Anderson, Indiana) emerged in the 1880s, and in early years perhaps 20 to 25 percent of ministers and delegates were women. John Smith, historian of the movement, has claimed that "forty years before the time of woman's suffrage on a national level, a great company of women were preaching, singing, writing, and helping to determine the policies in this religious reform movement" and that "it is probably safe to say that no other movement, either religious or secular, in this period of American history, except the suffrage movement itself, had such a high percentage of women leaders whose contribution was so outstanding."

The major product of the holiness revival was the Church of the Nazarene, whose 1894 founding constitution specifically provided for the right of women to preach. One entire conference from west Tennessee consisted for a time of only women ministers. Out of the Church of the Nazarene came in 1905 a book entitled *Women Preachers* that recorded the testimonies

and "calls to ministry" of a dozen such women. Early rolls of
Nazarene ministers indicate that perhaps 20 percent of the
clergy in this denomination were women.

The Pilgrim Holiness Church was similar. Founder Seth
Cook Rees (father of Paul S. Rees, prominent in the founding
of the National Association of Evangelicals in the 1940s)
worked with his wife as copastor and coevangelist. In setting
forth his vision for the new church, Rees exploded, "Nothing
but jealousy, prejudice, bigotry, and a stingy love for bossing in
men have prevented woman's public recognition by the church."
An early edition of the Pilgrim Holiness *Manual* indicates that
in some sections of the church as many as 30 percent of the
ordained ministers were women.

And the more sectarian the body, the firmer its feminist convictions. The most striking illustration of this is a minuscule
holiness denomination called the Pillar of Fire. This group was
founded by Alma White, wife of a Methodist minister. This
woman was consecrated bishop by her denomination, and she
claimed to be the first woman bishop in Christian history. Even
more interesting, for years this denomination published under
the editorship of Mrs. White a paper called *Woman's Chains*,
calling for the complete enfranchisement of women, their func-
tioning in Congress and the presidency, and other forms of
complete equality in both church and society.

Such were the feminist convictions of large sections of what
has come to be known as Evangelicalism. This heritage is almost totally lost today except where it was more firmly institutionalized, such as in the Salvation Army. Even those denominations most firmly committed to women in the ministry have
largely abandoned the practice. By 1973 the percentage of
women ministers in the church of the Nazarene had dropped to
about 6 percent. What was no doubt the most massive effort to
incorporate women into the life of the Christian church has
faded away and today is not even remembered.

9   Anointed to Preach
      the Gospel to the Poor

The Civil War marks a major point of transition in the Evangelical social consciousness. Some of the social and theological reasons for the shifts that took place will be developed in the next chapter. Here it is sufficient to note that pre–Civil War revivalism tended to split into two streams. On the more liberal side was the social gospel movement in which persons like Walter Rauschenbusch emerged from revivalism to apply christian principles to labor relations, urbanization, and so forth. Timothy Smith has argued in his still controversial book *Revivalism and Social Reform*[1] that the social gospel had strong roots in pre–Civil War revivalism and carried into the postwar era the broader themes of progress and hope for a Christian society. Whatever the validity of his thesis, it is the social gospel movement that has received the most attention from historians of the late nineteenth century. It has generally been assumed that the increasing polarizations within Protestantism that climaxed in the Fundamentalist/Modernist controversy of the 1920s and 1930s forced a split between those with a "social conscience" and those who advocated a "personal gospel" of individual regeneration.

This caricature contains some truth, but it is also a grave distortion. Just as the social gospel was a manifestation of a social conscience among theological liberals, there was also a disaffection with bourgeois church life among the more theologically conservative. This movement (in some ways more conservative and in some ways more radical than the social gospel)

1. Timothy L. Smith, *Revivalism and Social Reform in Mid-nineteenth Century America* (New York: Abingdon Press, 1957), esp. chap. 14.

drew its inspiration even more clearly from Finney's "new measure" revivalism. This little known aspect of American church life cries out for further study, not only to fill out the history of the period, but also for the illumination of current questions. This chapter can only provide hints of the material available for study.

Historians have wondered what happened to the abolitionist impulse after the Civil War. To some extent it died out with the emancipation of the slaves, though many Christians, sensitive to the broader problems of prejudice and injustice, devoted their lives to work among the freedmen. But the major force of the antislavery struggle was in the postwar era rechanneled into the "purity crusade" against prostitution. This movement captured the major figures in the antislavery struggle (from William Lloyd Garrison on down the line) and the rhetoric that had been used against slavery. Now the goal was to "abolish" (rather than regulate!) the "white slave trade" that supported the widespread prostitution of the era.

This purity crusade was closely tied to another issue held over from the pre–Civil War period—temperance reform. Here, too, the aim was not regulation but abolition—total abstinence and prohibition. Modern sympathy has been more with the antislavery struggle, which in a sense succeeded, than with the movement for prohibition, which was eventually rejected. This fact has obscured the character of temperance reform and its real parallels with the antislavery movement. Both campaigns sought a major restructuring of society. In the debate between "personal regeneration" and "cleaning up the environment" as approaches to moral and social rehabilitation, the temperance movement came out on the liberal side. It called for altering the environment so that people would not be subjected to the social problems attributed to alcohol.

But it is true that the purity crusade and the temperance movement were more amenable to a "personal morality" orientation. While the slaveholder was the sinner in the case of slavery, the prostitute and the drunkard were more directly engaged in sin and needed to be "rescued" from their plight. In these movements the broader social issues did drop into the background, though as we shall see this was not the whole story.

The purity crusade and temperance reform were at the time expressions of real concern for the outcasts of society. In this work Evangelicals in part acted in obedience to and in part discovered a basic affirmation of Scripture that is only now being reemphasized by the church. If there is a consistent theme in the activist movements in the church, from liberation theology to more traditional relief, it is the declaration of a special Christian responsibility to the poor and oppressed of this world. These movements proclaim that the Scriptures have a bias in favor of the economically poor. This concern is clear in the Gospel of Luke where Jesus quotes the prophet Isaiah to describe his own mission as being "anointed to preach the gospel to the poor" (Luke 4:18). The rest of the Gospel of Luke makes it clear that "poor" must be understood primarily in economic terms.

This theme appears regularly in the theologically conservative disaffection from bourgeois church life in the late nineteenth century. These Evangelicals understood this biblical teaching and gave themselves to the poor and the inner cities in response. This impulse was clearly grounded in the work of Finney and his friends. We have already seen (in chap. 6) how the New York churches under Finney's influence belonged to a separate Third Presbytery that consisted only of "free churches." These churches were so called because they were a self-conscious protest against the "renting" or selling of pews, a practice that grew in some circles as churches moved into the middle and upper classes and began to build more elaborate sanctuaries, in some cases modeled on a small scale on European cathedrals.

The Finneyites resisted this practice. Such rentals encouraged seating according to wealth and social class and thereby contradicted scriptural injunctions about being a "respecter of persons." Though some pews were usually left unassigned, to sit there was a sign of poverty and a public embarrassment that discouraged the poor from attending church and contributed to alienation between social classes. This practice seemed inconsistent with the teachings of Jesus that the church has a special responsibility to the poor.

The question of "free churches" continued to be a matter of contention in a variety of denominations in the middle decades of the nineteenth century. Usually the struggle was contained within each denomination with some churches insisting on "free seats" while others adopted a rental system. But in at least one case these questions made a major contribution to the emergence of a new denomination. In 1860 tensions in upstate New York led to the founding of the Free Methodist Church. The word *free* stood for a number of things, including abolitionism and the principle of "free pews."

The struggle over this issue was intense in the Methodist Episcopal Church which, though it had been primarily a lower-class or lower middle class church, was now rapidly rising into the upper middle class. The principle of "free seats" had been written into the Methodist Episcopal *Discipline* as follows: "Let all our churches be built plain and decent, and with free seats; but not more expensive than is absolutely unavoidable; otherwise ʻhe necessity of raising money will make rıch men necessary ɔ us. But if so, we must be dependent on them, yea, and governed by them. And then farewell to Methodist discipline, if not doctrine too."

But this rule was dropped in 1852, and the way was opened for the pew-rental system to be introduced into Methodism. In response to this decision and its broader implications for church life, the Free Methodist Church was born. A statement in an early *Discipline* of this group embedded this principle of "free seats" into the basic statement of purpose. "All their churches are required to be as free as the grace they preach. They believe that their mission is two-fold—to maintain the Bible Standard of Christianity—and to preach the Gospel to the poor. Hence they require that all seats in their houses of worship should *be free*."

The rest of this statement was taken from an article in the first issue of the *Earnest Christian*, edited by B. T. Roberts, founder of the denomination. In that editorial Roberts expresses

Orange Scott, founder of the Wesleyan Methodist Connection of America, an abolitionist denomination.

Luther Lee, early leader and theologian of the Wesleyan Methodists.

Antoinette Brown, graduate of Oberlin College and the first woman to be fully ordained to the Christian ministry.

Lay evangelist Phoebe Palmer, author of *The Promise of the Father* (1859), a major, early defense of the right of women to preach.

Amanda Smith, world renowned black woman evangelist of the late nineteenth century.

"The Purity Crusade": an early woodcut of the Salvation Army carrying into Parliament a two-mile-long petition to raise the age of consent to allow legal leverage against the "white slave trade."

Catherine Booth, cofounder of the Salvation Army and an ardent feminist.

William Booth, cofounder of the Salvation Army.

Waiting for Thy Coming.

"For the coming of the Lord draweth nigh."—James 5 : 8.

F. J. CROSBY.   IRA D. SANKEY.

1. We are waiting, blessed Sav-iour, We are watching for the hour,
2. We are waiting, blessed Sav-iour, We are watching, not in vain,
3. We are waiting, blessed Sav-iour, For a un-ion heart to heart,

When, in maj-es-ty de-scend-ing, Thou shalt come in mighty power;
For the cloud that bore Thee up-ward, And will bring Thee back a-gain,
With our dear ones o'er the riv-er, Where we nev-er more shall part;

Then the shadows will be lift-ed, And the darkness rolled a-way;
Then, a-mong Thy ransom'd peo-ple, We shall tread the shining way,
Then our sor-rows, in a mo-ment, Like a dream will pass a-way,

And our eyes be-hold the splen-dor Of the glorious crowning-day.
And our eyes be-hold the splen-dor Of the glorious crowning-day.
When our eyes be-hold the splen-dor Of the glorious crowning-day.

Turn-of-the-century gospel song, illustrating the rise of the premillennial eschatological views that tended to dilute the earlier Evangelical social reform vision.

his understanding of the class bias of the Scripture and appeals to the Lukan texts so popular today. "The provisions of the Gospel are for all. . . . *But for whose benefit are special efforts to be put forth?* Who must be *particularly* cared for? Jesus settles this question. He leaves no room for cavil. When John sent to know who he was, Christ charged the messengers to return and show John the things which they had seen and heard. 'The blind receive their sight, and the lame walk; the lepers are cleansed, and the deaf hear; the dead are raised up,' and, as if all this would be insufficient to satisfy John of his claims, he adds, 'AND THE POOR HAVE THE GOSPEL PREACHED TO THEM.' This was the crowning proof that He was the ONE THAT SHOULD COME."

Roberts insisted that "in this respect the Church must follow in the footsteps of Jesus. She must see that the gospel is preached to the poor." He also came very close to arguing that obedience to this example is *the* sign of the true church. "There are hot controversies about the true church. . . . It may be that there cannot be a church without a bishop, or that there can. There can be none without a gospel, and a gospel for the poor." Or again, "the poor are the favored ones. They are not called up. The great are called down."

The Free Methodists made this the determinative principle for the whole of church life. Roberts argued that "the edifice in which the gospel is preached should be built plain, and with all the seats free, with special reference to meeting the needs of the poor." Similarly, "the Free Methodist church requires all its members to dress plain. So plain people need not be afraid to attend church with them." Roberts pushed his followers to a radical discipleship that affirmed simple life-style, polemicized against the "modern, easy way of getting people converted, without repentance, without renouncing the world," and insisted that such renunciation of the world include such social sins as "slavery, driving hard bargains, and oppressing the hireling in his wages."

As the century wore on, such convictions became more wide-spread among Evangelicals. With the growth of cities, "preaching the gospel to the poor" involved a call to the inner-city districts and, more explicitly, to ministry in skid-row and red-light districts. A. B. Simpson, who came to New York's 13th Street Presbyterian Church in 1879, struggled for two years to turn this church outside itself to the poor of New York City and described the increasing polarization in these words: "What they wanted was a conventional parish for respectable Christians. What this young pastor wanted was a multitude of publicans and sinners."

Finally Simpson resigned, announcing his decision in an address based on the text "the Spirit of the Lord is upon me because he hath anointed me to preach the gospel to the poor." He then began a series of moves around the city that climaxed in founding the "Gospel Tabernacle" for immigrants located in the Times Square area. Out of Simpson's work grew the Christian and Missionary Alliance, a movement that originally understood itself to have a special call to serve the "neglected classes both at home and abroad."

The Church of the Nazarene was an interdenominational movement which brought together a number of people who shared the belief that it was the Christian's responsibility to minister to the poor. After years of service in some of the most beautiful churches and well-paid pulpits of California Methodism, Phineas F. Bresee felt called in the 1890s into ministry to the poor of inner-city Los Angeles. Bresee originally hoped to maintain his ministerial relationship in the Methodist conference while engaging in this work, but the bishop and his cabinet refused this request, forcing him to sever his lifelong relationship to found in 1895 the Church of the Nazarene.

The original "Articles of Faith and General Rules" described the "field of labor" of the new church as "the neglected quarters of the cities." The name Church of the Nazarene was chosen to symbolize "the toiling, lowly mission of Christ" by taking a "name which was used in derision of Him by His enemies." Like their predecessors in this succession, the Nazarenes adapted the whole of their church life to this mission. They objected to the wealth spent in elaborate churches, not only because such churches made the poor feel uncomfortable, but because the money used should have been spent to feed and clothe the hungry and the naked.

Illustrative of these sentiments is the following statement: "We want places so plain that every board will say welcome to the poorest. We can get along without rich people, but not without preaching the gospel to the poor. . . . Let the Church of the Nazarene be true to its commission; not great and elegant buildings; but to feed the hungry and clothe the naked, and wipe away the tears of sorrowing; and gather jewels for His diadem."

But such sentiments were not just Bresee's. Large parts of the denomination in the Southwest consisted of little more than chains of inner-city missions. One paper started in 1906 in Texas was called *Highways and Hedges*. Its title boldly proclaimed that "the respectable have had this call and rushed madly on after the things of this world" and claimed that "Steeple-house church people are busy chasing dollars . . . while some are too firmly married to their church creeds to listen to the call." This paper vowed to "open up a chain of missions in all of our large cities where real mission and slum work will be pushed; and the poor and the destitute looked after."

Similar convictions were echoed by A. M. Hills, the first systematic theologian of the new denomination. In preaching a sermon on "He Hath Anointed Me" from Luke 4:18–19, Hills said Jesus "was anointed to preach good tidings to the poor. An English writer has said that the oppression of the poor by the rich and powerful and their patience under oppressions and wrongs is ever the marvel of history. The poor were never appreciated until Christ came. . . . In the eyes of Christian law and of our country all men are on a common footing of rights and equality whatever their condition. Why? Because Jesus came to the poor, to preach the gospel to them, to tell them of their worth as men regardless of all accidents of birth, position, or race."

While groups like the Church of the Nazarene were in the beginning primarily a chain of rescue missions, this work did not always produce new denominations. Some institutions were supported by denominations as a part of their work in the inner cities, and other missions, like the famous Pacific Garden Mission in Chicago, were denominationally independent, deriving support from a number of sources. Usually such missions were located in skid-row areas and focused on the down-and-out alcoholic, providing meals, lodging, clothing, medical care, efforts at rehabilitation, and of course "salvation."

The origins of this movement are obscure, though there were antecedents in Europe, particularly in the work of Thomas Chalmers. But the earliest in America was a small mission with a single room in the Five Points district of Manhattan. Very often such institutions provided an outlet for women not able to minister in normal churches. This mission was started by a group of Methodist women, including evangelist Phoebe Palmer, who "were attracted to this place accompanied with an earnest desire to test the power of Christianity to give life even there." Their work was not without opposition. "They were told by gentlemen whom they requested to survey the ground, that no suitable room could be procured, but they expressed their determination to send a missionary there, which they did in 1850."

These women later raised money to buy an "Old Brewery," which was demolished for the building of a new "mission house." This mission worked with children as well as adults, holding several kinds of meetings and Sunday schools. Temperance societies were founded, and efforts were made to find employment. Plans were announced to build housing, to establish a hospital, to generate employment, and in other ways to serve the needs of this community.

But the most famous of the early rescue missions was the Water Street Mission, which was founded in 1872 by ex-convict Jerry McAuley and which became the model for scores of similar institutions around the world. Converted in the Water Street Mission was S. H. Hadley, the dominant figure in the movement. A. T. Pierson claimed that perhaps seventy-five thousand men were converted under Hadley's influence. Hadley's brother was also converted at the Water Street Mission and went on to found more than sixty rescue missions himself. Through these missions the Evangelical world of the age launched a major war against liquor.

Parallel to these rescue missions for men were institutions committed to work among "fallen women." Emma Whittemore founded the first Door of Hope in 1890, some fifteen years after being converted under the influence of Jerry McAuley at the Water Street Mission. Before Mrs. Whittemore's death, one hundred homes had been opened.

Similarly, in 1882 after the death of his five-year-old daughter, Charles Crittendon turned to such work and plowed into it the fortune he had made in the drug business. He named his missions the Florence Crittendon homes after his daughter, and the chain grew to some seventy-five. This was not easy work. The churches looked down on him for involving himself with such "unsavory" people, and much time had to be spent convincing respectable church people that women were often involved in prostitution out of economic necessity and kept it in because no one would help them get out or get jobs.

Many other manifestations of these themes could be mentioned, but their profoundest incarnation was the Salvation Army. This movement originated in England as the Christian Mission founded in the 1860s by William and Catherine Booth. This mission was a protest against "respectable churches" whose life cut them off from the masses. Its dominant concern was to follow Christ, "who, though he was rich, yet for our sakes became poor, that we, through his poverty, might become rich, and who has left us an example that we should follow in his steps."

The Salvation Army came to America about 1880 and by the end of the century had thousands of officers engaged in relief and evangelism throughout the cities of the world. A living critique of the bourgeois churches and a disturber of the peace by revealing the sickening underside of a supposedly respectable society, the army generated intense opposition from both mobs and church people. In one twelve-month period about 1880, 669 Salvationists were reported "knocked down, kicked, or brutally assaulted," 56 army buildings were stormed, and 86

Salvationists imprisoned (the mobs attacked, but the Salvationists were arrested and imprisoned).

Though primarily concerned with salvation and preaching the gospel to the poor, the Salvation Army, like other slum workers, soon found itself providing other services. Most immediate were the needs for food, clothing, and shelter. A "poor man's bank" was established. Day-care centers were provided to permit mothers to get out to earn a living for their families. The army discovered that the legal system was biased toward those who could afford to hire counsel, and it therefore provided free legal aid. Special attention was given to work among prisoners. The Army sought to become the custodian of first offenders to prevent their being sent to prisons that would turn them into hardened criminals. (Other work among prisoners yielded some unexpected dividends; one army post in 1896 reported that 47 of its 48 members had prison records!)

Prostitution was a particular concern of the army. The Booths startled many with sympathy for the prostitute, arguing that social conditions more than inherent evil forced young women into the "world's oldest profession." The Booths joined forces with muckraking journalist W. T. Stead to expose the white slave trade in which young girls were kidnapped, tricked, or sold into prostitution. Stead arranged for the purchase of a young virgin and wrote up the incident in his paper. The controversy resulted in Stead's imprisonment but forced Parliament to provide a legal weapon against the practice by raising the age of consent.

Stead carried this campaign to America and in 1894 published a book entitled *If Christ Came to Chicago*. This book must rank as a classic of Christian "investigative reporting." It named names and marshaled devastating facts and statistics. One appendix contained a "black list" that indicated not only the ostensible owner of each building in Chicago's red-light district, but also who really paid the taxes. The result was a major shake-up in Chicago.

The work of Stead and the Salvation Army shows the inadequacy of viewing these movements as conservative because they emphasized conversion. They incarnated egalitarian ideas about

women, for example, far in advance of their age and provided in
many cases an outlet for church women denied access to other
roles of ministry. These movements explicitly rejected the double standard of sexual ethics and generated sympathy for the
exploited prostitute. Their work did much to contribute to the
"discovery of poverty" in the late nineteenth century that supported the "progressive reforms." Personal understanding of the
conditions in the slums provided the basis for the support of
new legislation.

But even more striking is that close contact with the poor and
oppressed forced Salvationists and other slum workers into an
increasingly radical critique of American society. The Booths'
son Ballington argued that "we must have justice—more justice
. . . to right the social wrong by charity is like bailing the ocean
with a thimble. . . . We must adjust our social machinery so that
the producers of wealth become the owners of wealth." In a
biography of Catherine Booth, W. T. Stead called her a "Socialist, and something more" because she was "in complete revolt
against the existing order." And the army's primary organ the
War Cry asserted that the chief social evil in America was the
"unequal and unjust distribution of wealth."

The Booths followed closely the emergence of socialism and
related utopian visions and strongly affirmed elements of both.
As William Booth put it, "I say nothing against any short cut
to the Millennium that is compatible with the Ten Commandments. I intensely sympathize with the aspirations that lie behind all these socialist dreams . . . what these good people want
to do, I also want to do." But he feared that many schemes
were idealistic and actually avoided the immediate pressing
needs of the poor. He drew an interesting parallel with certain
forms of Christian theology. "This religious cant which rids
itself of all the importunity of suffering humanity by drawing
unnegotiable bills payable on the other side of the grave is not
more impracticable than the socialist clap-trap which postpones
all redress of human suffering until after the general overturn.
Both take refuge in the Future to escape a solution of the problems of the Present, and it matters little to the sufferers whether

the Future is on this side of the grave or the other. Both are, for them, equally out of reach."

The adequacy of that pragmatic turn of mind I shall leave to others to debate. The point here is to draw attention to a certain Evangelical protest against the bourgeois church of the late nineteenth century. This protest drew its inspiration from Christ's mission of "preaching the gospel to the poor." Obedience to that ideal forced those who followed it not only into various forms of social service and welfare work, but also to profound identification with the class interests of the poor and a consequent radical critique of existing society.

10 Whatever Happened to Evangelicalism?

The currents described in this book are, of course, not the whole of Evangelicalism. Extensive immigration producing various ethnic denominations occurred primarily in the post–Civil War period. Such church bodies followed their own dynamic and became subject to American influences late in the story traced here. Likewise, highly confessional churches in Lutheran and related traditions, though deeply influenced by American revivalism, show divergent patterns of development. And within major denominations, elements like the "Old School" or "Princeton Theology" within Presbyterianism (more about this later) set themselves firmly against the currents of revivalism and thus against the reforms that revivalism generated.

But these other traditions were not at the heart of American Evangelical experience in quite the same way as the currents traced in this book. Some of the other traditions have, in fact, been somewhat suspect from the viewpoint of "hardcore" Evangelicalism. The extent to which the movements described in this book lie behind the institutions of Evangelicalism may be seen, for example, when the editors of *Christianity Today* survey Christian colleges for responses to some topic of current discussion. A majority of such institutions will be rooted in churches and movements mentioned in this book.

What happened, then, to the reforming spirit of Evangelicalism? The answer is complex and perhaps can never be completely explained. Sociological, theological, historical, and psychological causes must be taken into account. This chapter is only an attempt at tentative explanation.

First is the difficulty of maintaining for a long period of time any movement with the intensity of, for example, the Oberlin commitment to the antislavery struggle. Those who have surveyed the dynamic of Christian social reform in America have noticed an ebb-and-flow pattern alternating between periods of creative vitality and periods of stability when gains are consolidated and institutionalized. To some extent these latter periods are also a reaction against reform and a return to other emphases of the Christian tradition. This pattern may be seen in recent years when the turbulent sixties gave way to the more tranquil and inner-directed styles of the seventies. From this perspective the surprising fact is that Oberlin, for example, was able to sustain its antislavery impulse from the mid-1830s through the Civil War.

But sociological interpretations of the dynamics of new movements also provide clues to the decline of Evangelical reform. The groups that we have surveyed were in large part products of revival and renewal efforts not unlike such earlier movements as Quakerism and Methodism. In some cases, these currents resulted in the formation of new sects; in others, they were contained within larger denominations as a leavening influence. Sociologists have described how such movements often turn to the poor and disinherited for support and in the process recover themes of "preaching the gospel to the poor." Such movements also make high ethical demands and require a rigorous dedication to an all-consuming mission.

Succeeding generations, however, find these concerns greatly diluted. A first generation gathers by conviction around highly motivating issues and devotes its resources to a narrowly defined set of goals. In the second generation, resources and attention are diverted to the education and nurture of children in the ways of the movement. This generation fails, however, to grasp the original vision with the same intensity and finds subtle ways to twist the movement's institutions to its own concerns. This process continues through several generations until in many cases the very opposite of what was originally intended is finally produced. This dynamic may be seen in the successive history of the movements described in this book.

Finney's revivalism also built strong barriers against the rest of the world—often with distinct behavioral patterns that set the "true believer" off from the rest of society. The revivalistic ethic of "no smoking, drinking, and dancing" functioned in part in this way, but children growing up under such restraints experience them primarily as factors alienating them from their peers and society. This experience produces an overwhelming desire to belong, to feel at home in the dominant culture. Where behavioral distinctions are not abandoned entirely, they are bent and twisted to permit what they were intended to prohibit. When they remain, they are usually only a faint echo of a whole dissenting value system now discarded in the rush to cultural accommodation.

A poignant example of this dynamic is the reaction of children to having mothers who were ministers. Many of my peers have mothers or grandmothers who were ministers, but this fact was hidden from friends as strange and abnormal. Only with the broader cultural shift of values on this question have they admitted that their mothers functioned in such roles.

Similar dynamics may be detected on the social and economic levels, especially if adherents to a movement are drawn from the lower economic classes—a natural result of hearing and obeying the biblical injunction to "preach the gospel to the poor." Discipline and a reordered life-style enable converts to rise in social class and economic level, a process culminating in a middle-class church like those against which the movement originally protested. This new church is subtly transformed into a bastion against those who would threaten its life, especially the lower classes that were once a source of vitality.

Sensitive leaders of such movements, often intuitively aware of this dynamic, have warned against the "dangers of riches" that undercut the original force of revival movements. John Wesley often commented on this problem. "Christianity, true scriptural Christianity, has a tendency, in the process of time, to undermine and destroy itself. For wherever true Christianity spreads, it must cause diligence and frugality, which, in the natural course of things, must beget riches! and riches naturally beget pride, love of the world, and every temper that is destructive of Christianity. . . . Wherever it generally prevails, it saps its own foundation."

But such general considerations ought not to obscure a number of unique factors that contributed to the decline of nineteenth-century Evangelical social involvement. The Civil War itself seems to have had a major impact. Finney's pre–Civil War revivalism was to some extent a reflection of the general optimism of the era that was a part of the youth of the nation and related to the seemingly endless frontiers to conquer. To Evangelicals of the 1830s and the 1840s it was inconceivable that good values should ever come into fundamental conflict with one another. Oberlinites, for example, were committed in early years to both the peace movement and the antislavery crusade. But when slavery proved to be more entrenched than expected and the struggle against it began to require violence, the Oberlinites had to choose between conflicting loyalties. In opting for the antislavery struggle, they discovered that the world was more complicated than they thought. The Civil War helped to puncture earlier utopian visions and in doing so contributed to the dissolution of the reform impulse.

The Civil War also resolved—at least on the surface—the most profoundly social of the reform issues that revivalism had supported. Left after the war were the temperance movement, the "purity crusade," the anti-Masonry campaign, and related issues. These concerns were more susceptible to translation into questions of personal morality detached from the larger social framework. As a result, one detects in the post–Civil War period a growing concern for personal purity, understood increasingly as "no smoking, no drinking, no dancing, and no gambling"—the elements that came to characterize the revivalistic ethic of later days.

But the post–Civil War era brought even profounder disappointments to the Evangelical dream. The revivalistic and reform movements had supported the broader expectation of a "Christian America" characterized by the incorporation into the legal and cultural life of the new nation of such principles as temperance, antislavery, Sabbath observance, and so on. Contemporary Evangelicalism has for the most part not given up this dream. The issues that really mobilize the opposition of, for example, the National Association of Evangelicals are efforts to delete references to God from the public life of the nation— Supreme Court decisions to outlaw official prayers in public schools or Madalyn Murray O'Hair's campaign to prevent astronauts from reading the Scriptures from space. Similarly, earlier generations of Evangelicals were deeply committed to blue laws and prohibition. Evangelicalism is still trying to cope with the fact that the United States has become a modern, secular, pluralistic state.

The post–Civil War period first began to force these questions on Evangelicalism. Waves of immigration brought, not only German Lutherans not inclined to follow the temperance banner, but also Roman Catholics and Jews who had no place (other than objects of conversion) in this dream of a Christian (read "Protestant"!) America. Massive urbanization and industrialization brought problems too complex for the revivalist reform vision. At the same time, attacks from without were intensified by the rise of biblical criticism, the emergence of Darwinism with its critique of the traditional view of human origins, and the difficulty of reconciling early chapters of Genesis with the new geological discoveries. Evangelicalism began to turn more and more in on itself to nurse the tattered remnants of the great vision for American life that had once thrust it out in aggressive reform.

Correlated with these issues were significant theological developments that reflected this pessimism and gave it additional strength. The first, and probably more important, of these developments took place in the doctrine of eschatology, the teaching about the events of the end-times. Pre–Civil War Evangelical eschatology was largely *postmillennial*, expecting Christ to return in judgment *after* a millennial reign of one thousand years. Post–Civil War Evangelical eschatology was dominated by a new doctrine of *premillennialism*. This view expected Christ to return *before* the millennium to take the saints out of this world in an event called the "rapture."

Finney's revivalism, as well as that of Jonathan Blanchard,

the Wesleyan Methodists, and other Evangelical reformers, was tied to postmillennialism. Reform activity was in part to prepare the way for the millennium, which was in turn a reflection of the vision of the "state of the perfect society" that drew Evangelicals into reform. Deeply intertwined was the Evangelical dream of a Christian America whose fullest manifestation would not be unlike the ushering in of the millennium.

But this vision collapsed after the Civil War and was replaced by an eschatology that looked for the return of Christ to rescue the "saints" *out of this world*. Premillennial teaching implied that the world was in such bad shape that it would only get worse until the return of Christ. Some even argued that efforts to ameliorate social conditions would merely postpone the "blessed hope" of Christ's return by delaying the process of degeneration. Premillennialism was articulated to the Evangelical world through conferences for the study of biblical prophecy that began in the 1870s and had a cumulative effect in the following decades. One major Evangelical leader after another announced his conversion to the new views. The postwar revivalism of evangelist D. L. Moody was, for example, closely tied to this new eschatology. By the 1920s Wheaton College, originally motivated by the postmillennial vision of Jonathan Blanchard, had written premillennial doctrines into a theological platform by which the college is today governed and to which the faculty is required to give annual subscription.

Implicit in these differing eschatological visions are widely divergent views of the way God effects the divine will in the world. The postmillennial teaching emphasizes the efficacy of God's grace and gradual progress under its influence. Pre–Civil War Evangelicals expected to live on this earth in the millennium and to enjoy the fruits of their labor. The premillennial vision, on the other hand, is more impressed with the power of sin and evil and the fact that this world will soon have to be abandoned for a heavenly abode.

Those conditioned to think that Evangelical theological discussions are resolved exclusively by scriptural exegesis would be astonished to discover the extent to which resolution of these eschatological issues depended upon matters of taste and perceptions of the direction in which the world was moving. Much of the appeal in the argumentation was to empirical evidence. The postmillennialists pointed to the progress of foreign missions and the spread of literacy to prove that the world was in fact getting better and better. Premillennialists, on the other hand, cited the rise of crime and social problems, often primarily in the cities, as evidence that the world was growing more evil. Apparently a great deal depended on reading these "signs of the times"!

This shift in eschatology had profound, and somewhat mixed, impact on the social involvement of Evangelicals. On the one hand, the expectation of the imminent return of Christ freed many from building for the immediate future (social advancement, pension plans, etc.) to give themselves wholeheartedly to the inner cities and foreign mission fields. Resulting contact with poor and oppressed peoples often pushed these devoted souls into relief and other welfare work—and occasionally into reform.

But more characteristic was the tendency to abandon long-range social amelioration for a massive effort to preach the gospel to as many as possible before the return of Christ. The vision was now one of rescue from a fallen world. Just as Jesus was expected momentarily on the clouds to rapture his saints, so the slum worker established missions to rescue sinners out of the world to be among those to meet the Lord in the air. Evangelical effort that had once provided the impulse and troops for reform rallies was rechanneled into exegetical speculation about the timing of Christ's return and into maintenance of the expanding prophecy conferences.

The extent to which this shift in eschatology was felt throughout Evangelical life and thought is difficult to overestimate. One of the most striking contrasts between pre–Civil War revivalists and those after the war is that the former founded liberal arts colleges while the latter established Bible schools. To the postwar premillennialist the liberal arts college involved too much affirmation of the cultural values of this world and took time away from the crucial task of getting a minimal knowledge of the Bible before rushing into the inner cities or the mission fields to gather as many souls as possible before the imminent return of Christ. In the late nineteenth century the Bible school movement picked up the message of the prophecy conferences and trained a whole generation of Evangelicals in the new doctrines. (One sign of how little premillennial eschatology really influences the practice of contemporary Evangelicals—in spite of the popularity of Hal Lindsey's best-selling interpretations of it—is seen in the fact that over the last generation many of these Bible schools have been gradually transformed into liberal arts colleges!)

But in addition to the rise of premillennialism, another major theological shift in Evangelicalism undercut the social reform of earlier years: the growth in impact among Evangelicals of the "Old School" of Presbyterianism, especially as it found expression in the "Princeton Theology." This theology is so called because it held sway at Princeton Theological Seminary from its founding in 1812 until the twentieth-century split that produced Westminster Theological Seminary. The Princeton Theology was grounded in Protestant scholasticism and represented the major articulation of the "Old Calvinism" against which Finney and his followers had reacted so strongly. The Princeton theologians, on their side, were horrified with both Finney's theology and his social views—as well as revivalism in general.

In the nineteenth century Finney's "New School" Presbyterian views dominated Evangelicalism, but the twentieth century has seen the increasing impact of the "Old School" Princeton Theology. This shift is widely discernible in Evangelicalism in the most surprising places. A striking example of this reversal may be seen in the history of Gordon College and Gordon-Conwell Theological Seminary, today the dominant Evangelical schools in New England. These schools are rooted in the work of A. J. Gordon, whose abolitionism and feminism we have already discussed. Though Baptist, Gordon stood very much in the tradition of Finney and, as such, was often the object of the sharp polemics of Benjamin B. Warfield, the major exponent of the Princeton Theology at the turn of the century. Yet more recently Gordon-Conwell has become one of the major advocacy centers of the Princeton Theology mediated through

Westminster Theological Seminary. Similar shifts occurred at Congregationalist Wheaton College, and by the 1950s even the Wesleyan Methodists were advocating certain formulations of the Princeton Theology.

The significance of such developments for Evangelical social reform is that the Princeton Theology incarnated extremely conservative social views. Charles Hodge, the major figure of this school said at the semicentennial celebration of his work at Princeton, "I am not afraid to say that a new idea never originated in this seminary." Though intended to speak of theology, this comment also indicates the conservative temperament of Hodge in other areas. He explicitly affirmed that the church should be a conservative force in society. Of the Presbyterian church he commented in 1861 that "we have preserved the integrity and unity of the Church, made it the great conservative body of truth, moderation, and liberty of conscience in our country."

This position pitted Hodge and the Princeton school firmly against Finney and the abolitionists. Hodge was disturbed by the abolitionist attack on so basic a structure of American society as slavery, insisting that Christianity was never "designed to tear up the institutions of society by its roots." In an attack on those like Finney who urged civil disobedience of the fugitive slave laws, he argued that the abolitionists were "a small minority of the people. They have never included in their ranks either the controlling intellect or moral feeling at the North. Their fundamental principle is anti-scriptural and therefore irreligious. They assume that slaveholding is sinful. This doctrine is the life of the sect. It has no power over those who reject that principle, and therefore it has not gained ascendancy over those whose faith is governed by the word of God." Hodge concluded that "both political despotism and domestic slavery, belong in morals to the *adiaphora*, to things indifferent."

Hodge did insist that slaveholders follow certain biblical norms that would moderate the extremes of slavery. He also hinted that over a long period of time education and moral training of slaves might so elevate them that emancipation would be appropriate. And when emancipation did come, he

supported it. But it is important to notice how Hodge's position
functioned in the antislavery struggle. His writings were used,
not only against the abolitionists, but also to defend slavery as
such. They appeared, for example, in *Cotton Is King, and Pro-
Slavery Arguments*, a major Southern defense of American
slavery.

Hodge and the Princeton school also opposed the women's
movement that emerged from abolitionism. Hodge argued that
"females and minors are judged (though for different reasons),
incompetent to the proper discharge of the duties of citizenship."
For Hodge there was "no form of human excellence before
which we bow with profounder deference than that which appears in a delicate woman adorned with the inward graces, and
devoted to the peculiar duties of her sex; and there is no de-
formity of human character from which we turn with deeper
loathing than from a woman forgetful of her nature and clam-
orous for the vocations and rights of men." Princeton theologians therefore opposed suffrage, arguing that the idea of two
autonomous votes in a single household was irreconcilable with
the biblical doctrine of the headship of the husband.

The contrast between the social positions of Finney and
Hodge has to be understood on several levels. There are hints of
social conditioning. Though Hodge opposed some of the church
structures that contributed to the situation, the Princeton Theology was more closely tied to the aristocracy and higher social
classes. While Finney was willing to cultivate these classes and
was proud of his success among them, his revivalism and his
social commitments drew him more to identification with the
poor, the slave, and the masses—at least to some extent. Both
Hodge and Finney, therefore, represented to a certain extent in
their thought the interests of those with whom they had aligned
themselves sociologically.

But such analysis is not adequate by itself and cannot explain, for example, the Tappan brothers. There were also fundamental differences in theology that can be correlated with the
divergent social positions. The Princeton Theology was a highly
intellectualized tradition that understood faith in a largely doc-

trinal sense and placed a high premium on orthodoxy and "right doctrine." While Oberlin was not antiintellectual and produced its own theology, it was more oriented to questions of ethics, action, and "right doing" or "right being."

Finney and Hodge also took significantly different positions on the question of determinism. Finney detested the determinism of "Old School Calvinism" and regularly denounced it. In affirming determinism, Hodge tended to argue that everything is done according to God's good purposes, and that whatever our position in life, we ought not to resist it, but find what good God wishes to work in that situation. In this view poverty becomes not only an unfortunate situation out of which God is able to bring good, but even more a result of a direct determination of God not to be resisted. Such a position not only supports the status quo but gives to it a divine endorsement.

But probably the most important theological distinction between Finney and Hodge was the relative emphasis they gave to sin and redemption. The Princeton theologians were deeply impressed by the presence of sin in the world. Hodge, for example, maintained that one implication of human depravity is that "no man, no community of men, no society, church or nation ever suffered in this life as much as their sins deserve. And, consequently, no individual or nation can ever justly complain of the dispensation of Divine providence as unmerited inflictions." The Princeton theologians also firmly resisted the idea of God's grace overcoming sin in this life. In doing this they came perilously close to making the sinful state a normative one.

Finney, on the other hand, placed greater weight on redemption and the power of God's grace to transform sinful persons and society. The significance of this shift is especially clear in discussions of the women's issue. Princeton theologians, deeply conscious of the impact of sin, tended to focus on the curse in the Genesis narrative of the Fall, arguing that the subordination of women in that passage provided a universal principle normative for all human life this side of the grave. Finney and the Oberlinites tended, on the other hand, to see the curse as descriptive of the sinful state out of which redemption is to be effected. In this perspective women may be elevated, especially in the church, to a position of equality.

In other words, Finney's emphasis on redemption provided that utopian edge necessary for a theology to support major social change. The importance of this theologically grounded utopianism has again become clear in recent discussions between the South American theologies of liberation and the school of Christian Realism that has dominated much recent American theology. Christian Realists find the liberation theologians' use of utopianism visionary and unrealistic. The Latin American theologians reply that without this theme the positions of the Christian Realists become in effect "ideologies of the establishment."[1] By analogy, Hodge was in his time a very conservative "Christian Realist" whose theology served as an "ideology of the establishment." Though accused of perfectionism by the Princeton theologians, Finney and his followers found in the doctrine of redemption the utopian vision that enabled them to press toward a society free of slavery and the subordination of women.

These theological insights also help us to understand how the Princeton Theology gained ascendancy in the Evangelical world. It incarnated the same tendency toward pessimism that was in premillennialism. Ernest Sandeen has argued in his *Roots of Fundamentalism* that the "biblical literalism" underlying both the prophecy conference movement and Princeton Theology doctrinalism formed the bridge by which the two movements were able to coalesce in the late nineteenth century into a mixture that laid the basis for modern Fundamentalism.[2] What is suggested here is that a common tendency toward a pessimistic world view was another bridge that permitted this coalescing.

1. For an overview of this discussion, see the foreword by William Lazareth to José Míguez Bonino, *Doing Theology in a Revolutionary Situation* (Philadelphia: Fortress Press, 1975).
2. Ernest R. Sandeen, *The Roots of Fundamentalism: British and American Millenarianism, 1800–1930* (Chicago: University of Chicago Press, 1970).

If there is any validity to the analysis of the differing social contexts that lay behind the Princeton and Oberlin theologies, that analysis suggests that as the movements and denominations formed in response to nineteenth-century revivalism rose socially and economically, they found the Princeton views more congenial to their new social positions. As they climbed higher in the social structure and became more and more a part of the established order, the Princeton Theology would have been more attractive precisely because it could function as an "ideology of the establishment."

And again, sociologists have described how movements that concentrate on ethics and religious experience in the first generation often shift to doctrine in succeeding generations. This movement from "being" and "doing" to "believing" could also support a new openness to the emphases of the Princeton theologians. Whatever the precise cause, it is clear that one can trace in Evangelicalism a growing emphasis on "right doctrine" as the measure of acceptability and a consequent shift away from religious experience and behavioral norms.

A final possible reason for the twentieth-century ascendancy of the Princeton Theology in Evangelicalism may be the rise of biblical criticism. The Princeton theologians had early on marshaled their forces to build a doctrine of "biblical inerrancy" adequate to resist the rising tides of criticism. Other traditions less well prepared for this struggle reached for the Princeton formulations and in the process incorporated other theological and social perspectives of the school.

But whatever the precise reasons for the rise of the Princeton Theology and its coalescing with the new premillennial doctrines, in this process we see both the rise of fundamentalism and the decline of Evangelical social involvement. This development is summarized by Otto Piper of a later day at Princeton in discussing the contributions of various nations to the development of Christian ethics. He suggests that "characteristic of American church life is a succession of nationwide ethical campaigns, in which the interest is focussed on the abolition of some single evil, for instance the emancipation of the slaves, prohibition of alcoholic beverages, pacifism, or, recently, civil

rights for the negroes. A contribution of lasting significance was
made by Finney's (1792–1875) insistence on holiness. He did
not only denounce the depravity of the sinner, as was common
in the revival movements, but also pointed out the blessings of
the Spirit's sanctifying power, by which a person's conduct is
radically transformed. In turn, the one-sided predilection which
Dispensationalism and Fundamentalism showed for theological
correctness was not conducive to the development of ethical
responsibility."[3]

In the Fundamentalist/Modernist controversy and in succeeding decades, the sociological, theological, and historical currents
produced a movement that in many ways stood for the opposite
of what an earlier generation of Evangelicals had affirmed.
What had begun as a Christian egalitarianism was transformed
into a type of Christian elitism. Revivalistic currents that had
once been bent to the liberation of the slave now allied themselves with wealth and power against the civil rights movement.
Churches and movements that had pioneered a new role for
women became the most resistant to contemporary movements
seeking the same goals.

In the process the rewriting of history began to take place.
Modern Evangelical editors of Finney's writings proceeded to
edit out references to social reform. When a 1900 biography of
evangelist Dwight L. Moody was reissued in 1930, some significant alterations had been made. The first edition reported that
in the Civil War Moody "could not conscientiously enlist" because "There has never been a time in my life when I felt I
could take a gun and shoot down a fellow being. In this respect
I am a Quaker." But the later edition, published at a time in
which pacifism was further from Evangelical thinking, reports
that Moody refused to serve because he had "dedicated himself
to Christian service"—implying that a "higher calling" rather
than conscientious scruples was his reason.[4] In 1943 the Wesleyan Methodists celebrated the one-hundredth anniversary of

---

3. Otto Piper, *Christian Ethics* (London: Thomas Nelson, 1970), p. 21.
4. These alterations are detected by Guy Franklin Hershberger, *The
Way of the Cross in Human Relations* (Scottdale, Penn.: Herald Press,
1958), chap. 8.

their founding with a special issue of the *Wesleyan Methodist*. But one has to search diligently for any reference to the slavery issue that brought the movement into existence. The reader is left with the impression that a group of highly spiritual men spontaneously came together to found a new denomination to lift up anew the spiritual message of the Wesleyan Revival as the fullest expression of New Testament truth.

Thus a great heritage of Evangelical social witness was buried and largely forgotten, and the stage was set for the ironic struggles of the 1960s in which the spiritual descendents of earlier Evangelical social activists would reject the modern manifestations of the reform impulse as inherently unbiblical and opposed to the spirit of Evangelical Christianity.

Epilogue:
Reflections on
Some Unresolved Issues

This study leaves many unresolved issues, most beyond the scope of this book. Questions of eschatology or the choice of competing theological systems cannot be resolved by history or by the extent to which such positions contribute to, or undermine, Christian social witness, though such considerations would surely play a part in the process. Nor can the Evangelical heritage here discovered be appropriated directly for our age without careful rethinking of important exegetical and theological questions or without careful analysis of the differences between the nineteenth and twentieth centuries. But the material surveyed in this book not only helps one to understand contemporary Evangelicalism but also calls into question some of the basic categories by which it is usually interpreted.

The history related in this book has, for example, forced me even to understand the word "Evangelical" in new ways. Today this label generally derives its connotations from the Fundamentalist/Modernist controversy of the early decades of this century. In the 1940s a second generation of Fundamentalists called themselves "Evangelicals" in part to project a more positive image. When used by this "post-Fundamentalist" party, the word is understood largely in terms of paradigms like the struggle within Presbyterianism that climaxed in the founding of Westminster Theological Seminary, an effort to preserve intact the Princeton Theology of the nineteenth century. According to this understanding the Fundamentalist or Evangelical is one who holds true to orthodox Christian faith (usually very narrowly defined) over against those who have diluted it by the acceptance of biblical criticism, evolution, the social gospel, and other modern liberal currents.

With the intellectual ascendency within contemporary Evangelicalism of the "post-Fundamentalist" party, the whole has come more and more to be understood in terms of this analysis. This perspective is clearly apparent, for example, in a recent interpretation entitled *The Evangelicals*. In an introductory essay delineating the "Theological Boundaries of Evangelical Faith," church historian John Gerstner equates Evangelicalism with the "Princeton school which had come to be recognized as nineteenth-century standard-bearer of evangelical orthodoxy." Clearly reflecting the nineteenth-century antipathy between Oberlin and Princeton (as indicated in the last chapter), Gerstner then finds that "Finney, the greatest of nineteenth-century evangelists, became the greatest of nineteenth-century foes of evangelicalism."[1]

The rise of this perspective has not only contributed to the decline of Evangelical social witness, as indicated in the preceding chapter, but has also tended to distort Evangelical historiography. Much more of modern Evangelicalism would stand, historically at least, in the succession of Finney and Oberlin than Hodge and Princeton. And when American church historians use the term "Evangelical," they generally refer to the emergence of the Arminian, pietistic revivalism that was epitomized in Finney and marked the end of the cultural dominance of the "Old Calvinism" preserved in the Princeton Theology and many modern post-Fundamentalist Evangelicals. Ironically this nineteenth-century Evangelicalism was highly motivated by a self-conscious repudiation of what has come to be the dominant theological system in modern Evangelicalism.

The importance of distinguishing these two types of Evangelicalism can be seen on several levels.[2] In spite of a great deal of overlap the two types focus on different areas of major concern. We have seen some of this in the contrasts between Oberlin and Princeton in the last chapter. The modern type of Evangelicalism with its roots in Princeton places a premium on "right doctrine" and the preservation of a particular brand of "orthodoxy." Eighteenth and nineteenth century Evangelicalism, on the other hand, was more concerned with the personal appropriation of grace—with conversion and the "new life" that follows the "new birth." These Evangelicals, though

1. David F. Wells and John D. Woodbridge, *The Evangelicals: What They Believe, Who They Are, Where They are Changing* (Nashville: Abingdon Press, 1975), pp. 28–29.

2. For a helpful confirmation of this distinction see the sharp polemic against the label "conservative Evangelical" by Presbyterian Ralph Winter of Fuller Theological Seminary in the introduction to his anthology, *The Evangelical Response to Bangkok* (South Pasadena, Calif.: William Carey Library, 1973). Winter understands Evangelicalism primarily in terms of the nineteenth-century type I am describing here.

not unorthodox in a broader sense, emphasized that Christian faith
that lacks vitality or is "unrevived" comes in several varieties, including orthodox. John Wesley, for example, never tired of affirming that "neither does religion consist in orthodoxy or right opinions.
. . . A man may be orthodox in every point. . . . He may be almost
as orthodox as the Devil . . . and may, all the while, be as great a
stranger as he to the religion of the heart."

This contrast can, of course, be overdrawn. The earlier Evangelicals were not without a concern for the preservation of genuine
Christianity, and modern Evangelicals certainly stress Christian Experience. But differing accents had profound social consequences.
It was revivalist Evangelicalism that supported the antislavery movement and opened up new roles for women. Even modern post-Fundamentalist Evangelicals usually point to the Evangelical Revival in
England or to pre–Civil War revivalism as the prime examples of
Evangelical social involvement, though generally without showing
awareness of the differences between revivalism and Fundamentalism.

But rejection of the modern Fundamentalist paradigm of Evangelicalism has also required another shift in categories of analysis.
As illustrated in the preceding chapter, full understanding of revivalistic Evangelicalism has required the incorporation of historical
and sociological categories into the theological analysis usually offered by adherents of modern Evangelicalism. The revivalist movement incarnated an element of protest against nominal Christianity
and the traditional churches that sometimes manifested itself in a
rather sectarian dynamic. If one is to judge by either the membership of the National Association of Evangelicals or by the movements that lie behind the colleges and seminaries recommended in
the pages of *Christianity Today*, much of contemporary Evangelicalism is rooted in the various sects, renewal movements, and new
denominations spawned in the wake of nineteenth-century revivalism.

These currents require sociological categories for full interpretation. It is possible to detect in such movements a certain centrifugal
movement in which these protest and revival forces spin out from
the patterns of traditional church life (hierarchical structures, li-
turgical worship, a trained clergy class, broad cultural affirmation,
and so forth) to a more egalitarian, spontaneous, lay-oriented, and
narrowly focused style of church life. The result is often a highly
innovative, but culturally marginal, movement identified with the

disenfranchised of society. But this centrifugal movement is usually followed by a corresponding but opposite centripetal movement back toward the center and affirmation of more traditional forms of church life, trained clergy, more elaborate worship, establishment values, and so forth.

Once discerned this dynamic greatly illumines the ironies of the history sketched in this book. Movements whose egalitarian thrust once manifested itself in feminism and abolitionism have in more recent years moved back toward more traditional patterns of church life and social views. One reason for the intense clash of the Evangelical world with the rise of the social movements of the 1960s was that the post–World War II generation of Evangelicals was at the height of its "centripetal" thrust. Evangelicalism was moving toward the center just as secularized centrifugal countercultural movements were spinning off in the opposite direction.

This centrifugal/centripetal dynamic also helps to explain a surprising number of phenomena in the contemporary Evangelical world. The recent amazing growth of Evangelical theological seminaries has been much analyzed in the religious press, and a variety of possible reasons have been advanced. What has not been noticed is that the Evangelical seminaries are vigorous and expanding because they are in many cases a century younger than the more established seminaries and are rooted largely in the post–World War II Evangelical rediscovery of theological education and the values of a trained clergy. Bethel Theological Seminary and Trinity Evangelical Divinity School are supported by small ethnic churches produced by nineteenth century revivalist and free church currents. Asbury Theological Seminary represents not so much the "orthodox" party within Methodism as the nineteenth century holiness movement that emerged from revivalist sources. Gordon-Conwell is probably best understood as the product of similar phenomena within Baptist contexts. Even interdenominational Fuller Theological Seminary in California fits the patterns of the other seminaries in terms of growth patterns and post–World War II founding.

This same centrifugal/centripetal dynamic also helps explain some of the tensions surfacing among those persons calling for a renewal of Evangelical social concern. For some this is a further step in moving toward the center. These persons call for a "responsible" social witness grounded in broader cultural affirmation correlatable with upward social mobility. But it is also possible to discern among other Evangelicals a renewal of the "centrifugal" thrust in protest against, and repudiation of, an Evangelicalism that has become bourgeois and establishment oriented. One often finds among these persons themes of restoration and renewal (and even occasionally a call for restoration of the "New Testament church"), a tendency toward communitarian and other countercultural life-styles, a willingness to draw on the charismatic renewal movements, frequent withdrawal from traditional churches to found house church movements, and so forth. This protest against the bourgeois church has many similarities to patterns of nineteenth-century sectarianism.

So far these conflicting thrusts are intermingled, often within the same groups and even within individuals. But evidence of a certain sorting out process continues to accumulate, and soon we may be able to discern whether the current calls for a renewal of Evangelical social witness are the final steps in the "maturation" (or "decline," depending on one's perspective) of Evangelicalism, or perhaps the first steps of new protest movements not unlike those of the nineteenth century, though no doubt given different shape and character by the new context of the twentieth century.

Bibliography

1. Jonathan Blanchard: The Radical Founder of Wheaton College

Blanchard, Jonathan, and Rice, N. L. *A Debate on Slavery*. Cincinnati: Moore, 1846. This book has been recently reprinted by Arno Press of the *New York Times*, Negro History Press, and Negro Universities Press.

Blanchard, Jonathan. *Sermons and Addresses*. Chicago: National Christian Association, 1892.

Kilby, Clyde. *Minority of One: The Biography of Jonathan Blanchard*. Grand Rapids: William B. Eerdmans, 1959.

Wyeth, Willard W. *Fire on the Prairie: The Story of Wheaton College*. Wheaton: Van Kampen Press, 1950.

2. Reform in the Life and Thought of Evangelist Charles G. Finney

Cole, Charles C., Jr. *The Social Ideas of the Northern Evangelists, 1826–1860*. New York: Columbia University Press, 1954.

Finney, Charles G. *Lectures on Revivals of Religion*. Edited by William G. McLoughlin. Cambridge: Belknap Press of Harvard University Press, 1960.

McLoughlin, William G. *Modern Revivalism: Charles G. Finney to Billy Graham*. New York: Ronald Press, 1959.

Rosell, Garth M. "Charles Grandison Finney and the Rise of the Benevolence Empire." Ph.D. dissertation, University of Minnesota, 1971. Available from University Microfilms, Ann Arbor, Michigan, order #72–14,448.

Vulgamore, Melvin L. "Social Reform in the Theology of Charles Grandison Finney." Ph.D. dissertation, Boston University, 1963. Available from University Microfilms, Ann Arbor, Michigan, order #64–391.

3. Theodore Weld: Evangelical Reformer

Barnes, Gilbert Hobbs. *The Anti-Slavery Impulse, 1830–1844*. New York: Appleton-Century Co., 1933. Also available in Harbinger paperback.

Barnes, Gilbert Hobbs, and Dumond, Dwight L., ed. *Letters of Theodore Dwight Weld, Angelina Grimké Weld and Sarah Grimké, 1822–44.* 2 vols. New York: Appleton-Century, 1934. Reprinted by Peter Smith of Gloucester, Massachusetts.

Thomas, Benjamin P. *Theodore Weld: Crusader for Freedom.* New Brunswick: Rutgers University Press, 1950. Reprinted in 1972 by Octogon Press.

Weld, Theodore. *The Bible Against Slavery.* New York: American Anti-Slavery Society, 1937. Reprinted in 1970 by Negro History Press of Detroit.

————. *Slavery As It Is.* New York: American Anti-Slavery Society, 1839. Reprinted in paperback as *American Slavery As It Is* by Arno Press; edited by Richard Curry and Joanna Dunlap Cowden as *Slavery in America.* Itasca, Ill.: F. E. Peacock, 1972.

4. The "Lane Rebellion" and the Founding of Oberlin College

Fairchild, James H. *Oberlin: The College and the Colony, 1833–1883.* Oberlin: E. J. Goodrich, 1883.

Fletcher, Robert S. *A History of Oberlin College from Its Foundation through the Civil War.* 2 vols. Oberlin: Oberlin College, 1943. This set reprinted by Books for Libraries.

Henry, Stuart C. "The Lane Rebels: A Twentieth Century Look." *Journal of Presbyterian History,* Spring 1971, pp. 1–14.

————. *Unvanquished Puritan: A Portrait of Lyman Beecher.* Grand Rapids: William B. Eerdmans, 1973. Chaps. 10 and 11 are on the "Lane Rebellion."

5. Civil Disobedience and the Oberlin-Wellington Rescue Case

Hosmer, William. *The Higher Law.* Auburn: Derby and Miller, 1852. Reprinted in 1969 by Negro Universities Press.

Madden, Edward H. *Civil Disobedience and Moral Law in Nineteenth-Century American Philosophy.* Seattle: University of Washington Press, 1968. Also available in a paperback edition.

Shipherd, Jacob R. *History of the Oberlin-Wellington Rescue.* Boston: J. P. Jewett, 1859. Reprinted in 1972 by DaCapo Press of New York in their series "Civil Liberties in American History."

6. Arthur and Lewis Tappan: The Businessman as Reformer

Abel, Annie Heloise, and Klingberg, Frank J. *A Side-light on Anglo-American Relations 1839–1858.* Washington, D.C.: The Association for the Study of Negro Life and History, 1927. Reprinted in 1970 by Augustus Kelley of New York.

Owens, William. *Black Mutiny: The Revolt on the Schooner Amistad.* Philadelphia: Pilgrim Press, 1968.

Tappan, Lewis. *The Life of Arthur Tappan.* New York: Hurd and Houghton, 1870. Reprinted in 1970 by Arno Press of the *New York Times.*

Wyatt-Brown, Bertram. *Lewis Tappan and the Evangelical War against Slavery.* Cleveland: The Press of Case Western Reserve University, 1969. Also available in Atheneum paperback.

7. Orange Scott, Luther Lee, and the Wesleyan Methodists

The Autobiography of the Rev. Luther Lee. New York: Phillips and Hunt, 1882.

Dayton, Donald W., ed. *Five Sermons and a Tract by Luther Lee.* Chicago: Holrad House, 1975.

Mathews, Donald G. "Orange Scott: The Methodist Evangelist As Revolutionary," In *The Antislavery Vanguard: New Essays on the Abolitionists.* Edited by Martin Duberman. Princeton: Princeton University Press, 1965. Also available in paperback edition.

———. *Slavery and Methodism: A Chapter in American Morality, 1780–1845.* Princeton: Princeton University Press, 1965.

Matlack, L. C. *The Life of the Rev. Orange Scott.* New York: C. Prindle and L. C. Matlack, 1847. Reprinted by Books for Libraries, 1971.

Scott, Orange. *The Grounds of Secession from the M. E. Church.* New York: C. Prindle, 1848. Reprinted by Arno Press of the *New York Times,* 1969.

8. The Evangelical Roots of Feminism

Dayton, Lucille Sider, and Dayton, Donald W. " 'Your Daughters Shall Prophesy': Feminism in the Holiness Movement." *Methodist History,* January 1976, pp. 67–92.

Gordon, A. J. "The Ministry of Women." Gordon-Conwell Monograph #61 with an introduction by Pamela Cole. A 16-page mimeograph reprint from *Missionary Review of the World,* December 1894, pp. 910–21.

Kraditor, Aileen S. *Up from the Pedestal: Selected Writings in the History of American Feminism.* Chicago: Quadrangle Books, 1968. Also available in paperback.

Lerner, Gerda. *The Grimké Sisters from South Carolina: Pioneers for Women's Rights and Abolition.* New York: Houghton Mifflin Company, 1967.

Olson, Della E. "A Woman of Her Times." A series of six essays in *The Evangelical Beacon,* 27 May 1975–2 September 1975.

Roberts, B. T. *Ordaining Women.* Rochester, N.Y.: Earnest Christian Publishing House, 1891.

Rossi, Alice. *The Feminist Papers.* New York: Columbia University Press, 1973. Also available in Bantam paperback.

Starr, Lee Anna. *The Bible Status of Women.* New York: Fleming Revell, 1926. Still in print with Zarephath, N.J.: Pillar of Fire, 1955.

9. Anointed to Preach the Gospel to the Poor

Booth, William. *In Darkest England and the Way Out.* London: International Headquarters of the Salvation Army, 1890. Still in print.

Brickley, Donald P. *Man of the Morning: The Life and Work of Phineas F. Bresee.* Kansas City, Mo.: Nazarene Publishing House, 1960.

Cole, Charles C., Jr. "The Free Church Movement in New York City," *New York History,* July 1953, pp. 284–97.

Heasman, Kathleen. *Evangelicals in Action: An Appraisal of Their Social Work in the Victorian Era.* London: Geoffrey Bles, 1962.

Magnuson, Norris. "Salvation in the Slums: Evangelical Welfare Work, 1865–1920." Ph.D. dissertation, University of Minnesota, 1968. Available from University Microfilms, Ann Arbor, Michigan, order #69–1548.

Roberts, B. T. *Pungent Truths.* Chicago: Free Methodist Publishing House, 1912. Reprinted Salem, Ohio: H. E. Schmul, 1973.

Stead, William T. *If Christ Came to Chicago.* Chicago: Laird & Lee, 1894.

10. Whatever Happened to Evangelicalism?

Barker, William S. "The Social Views of Charles Hodge (1797–1878): A Study in 19th-Century Calvinism and Conservatism." *Presbyterion,* Spring 1975, pp. 1–22.

Elliott, E. N., ed. *Cotton Is King, and Pro-Slavery Arguments.* Augusta, Ga.: Pritchard, Abbott & Loomis, 1860. Reprinted New York: Johnson Reprint Corporation, 1968.

Hogeland, Ronald W. "Charles Hodge, the Association of Gentlemen and Ornamental Womanhood: A Study of Male Conventional Wisdom, 1825–1855," *Journal of Presbyterian History*, Fall 1975, pp. 239–55.

Moberg, David. *The Great Reversal: Evangelism versus Social Concern.* Philadelphia: J. B. Lippincott Company, 1972.

Sandeen, Ernest R. *The Roots of Fundamentalism: British and American Millenarianism, 1800–1930.* Chicago: University of Chicago Press, 1970.

DATE DUE

JOSTEN'S 30 508